AF431767

# Crock Pot Cookbook

## Healthy and Delicious Recipes for Your Slow Cooker

### Melanie Bennet

© **Text Copyright 2022 by Melanie Bennet - All rights reserved.**

This document is geared towards providing exact and reliable information in regards to the topic and issue covered. The publication is sold with the idea that the publisher is not required to render accounting, officially permitted, or otherwise, qualified services. If advice is necessary, legal or professional, a practiced individual in the profession should be ordered.

From a Declaration of Principles which was accepted and approved equally by a Committee of the American Bar Association and a Committee of Publishers and Associations.

In no way is it legal to reproduce, duplicate, or transmit any part of this document in either electronic means or in printed format. Recording of this publication is strictly prohibited and any storage of this document is not allowed unless with written permission from the publisher. All rights reserved.

The information provided herein is stated to be truthful and consistent, in that any liability, in terms of inattention or otherwise, by any usage or abuse of any policies, processes, or directions contained within is the solitary and utter responsibility of the recipient reader. Under no circumstances will any legal responsibility or blame be held against the publisher for any reparation, damages, or monetary loss due to the information herein, either directly or indirectly.

Respective authors own all copyrights not held by the publisher.

The information herein is offered for informational purposes solely, and is universal as so. The presentation of the information is without contract or any type of guarantee assurance.

The trademarks that are used are without any consent, and the publication of the trademark is without permission or backing by the trademark owner. All trademarks and brands within this book are for clarifying purposes only and are owned by the owners themselves, not affiliated with this document.

# Table of Contents

## CHAPTER FOUR



## CHAPTER FIVE

## CHAPTER SIX

## CHAPTER SEVEN



## CHAPTER EIGHT

# CHAPTER ONE

# Introduction of the Crock Pot

A Crock Pot is a slow cooker initially developed by the Naxon Corporation. When the company was purchased by The Rival Company, the product was introduced with the Crock Pot name in 1971. Its popularity began in the 1970s and has increased over the decades.

While designs vary, a Crock Pot consists of a ceramic pot with a glass lid. The removable pot is placed inside a metal housing. The electric heating element is in the housing. As a Crock Pot is available in many sizes, you can find the perfect pot for every household.

Modern Crock Pots offer more features than the slow cookers of the distant past. Heat settings are one example. Depending on the foods you are cooking and your personal preferences, you can set the pot to low or high. Some pots also have a setting to keep food warm after it has cooked.

Some advanced models have a browning feature handy when cooking meat. Some newer models also offer timers. The temperature will lower when the food reaches a certain temperature. This option allows you to control cooking temperatures even when you are not home.

## Benefits of Using a Crock Pot

For most people, the most important benefit of a Crock Pot is convenience. Using one pot to cook an entire meal is easier than cooking with several pots and pans. A full meal can be prepared in just a few minutes. People who have full-time jobs, attend school, or have other time-consuming responsibilities can start the meal in the morning and know it will be ready to eat when they come home.

A Crock Pot is much safer than traditional stoves and ovens. Using a Crock Pot correctly will not risk being burned, and there is no fire risk.

Saving money is another benefit. You do not need to buy expensive cuts of your favorite meats because cheaper cuts will become tender, and the meat will never be tough or dry. You will also save money because washing a Crock Pot uses much less water than washing many pots and pans.

Personal taste is an additional benefit of slow cookers. When the flavors of all the foods in the pot blend, you will have a delicious meal.

## How to Use a Crock Pot

It is always wise to read the instructions on a new appliance, but a slow cooker is quite simple.

**First, consider safety.** Make sure your outlet and wiring are in good condition so that the pot will not be a fire hazard. Always use the pot on a clean, dry surface, and never allow the cord to come in contact with water.

Do not allow children to play near the pot or open it to peek inside. The steam from a slow cooker is hot. Exercise care when you open the pot and remove the food. As the liquid is very hot, it is easy to burn yourself if you are not careful.

Use the amount of water recommended in the recipe. Never fill the pot with water.

**Second, familiarize yourself with the settings.** The Low setting is generally used for foods you wish to simmer. The High setting is for foods you would normally fry, boil, or bake. High is the appropriate setting for meats, stews, desserts, and most recipes. The warm setting is intended to keep food warm after it is cooked.

**A third consideration is cleaning and maintaining your Crock Pot.** As the pot rarely requires maintenance, all you need to do is clean it after use. While you can wash the pot and lid in the sink, never immerse the metal housing in water. If food or other residues need to be removed from the housing, use a moist cloth after unplugging the appliance.

## Tips for Crock Pot Cooking

A Crock Pot does not cause water to evaporate. If you are not using a recipe specially created for slow cookers, only add enough water to cover the food.

For the most flavorful dishes, try the low setting. Food will cook completely in the gentle heat.

If the dish you are making includes rice or pasta, add it shortly before the other ingredients have finished cooking. Texture and taste will be better.

Feel free to experiment with your Crock Pot. In this book, you will find 105 healthy and delicious Crock Pot recipes that each contain nutritional information. With a bit of practice, you will see that virtually every food you like can be cooked in this appliance.

# CHAPTER TWO

# Breakfast

## Apple French Toast Casserole

**Servings:** 6
**Cooking Time:** 8 hours
**Ingredients:**
5 eggs
¾ cup half-and-half
¾ cup milk
¼ cup brown sugar, divided
1¾ teaspoons ground cinnamon
1 teaspoon vanilla extract
Pinch of salt
8 whole-grain bread slices, halved diagonally
3 medium apples, peeled, cored, and sliced thinly
¼ cup almonds, toasted and chopped

**Directions:**
1. Lightly grease the Crock Pot with nonstick cooking spray.
2. In a bowl, add eggs, half-and-half, milk, 3 tablespoons of brown sugar, cinnamon, vanilla extract, and salt, and beat until well combined.
3. Arrange the bread slices in the bottom of the prepared Crock Pot.
4. Place the apple slices over the bread slices. Pour the egg mixture evenly over the apple slices.
5. Sprinkle with the remaining brown sugar.
6. Set the Crock Pot on Low. Cover and cook for about 6–8 hours.

7. Uncover and set aside to cool for about 20 minutes before serving.

8. Cut into slices of equal size, and serve with a topping of almonds.

**Nutritional Information (Per Serving)**
Calories: 301
Fat: 11.2 g
Sat Fat: 4.2 g
Carbohydrates: 42.6 g
Fiber: 6.2 g
Sugar: 22.1 g
Protein: 11.7 g
Sodium: 308 mg

# Breakfast Casserole

**Servings:** 8
**Cooking Time:** 7–8 hours
**Ingredients:**
12 large eggs
1 cup milk
Salt and pepper to taste
1 cup green bell pepper, chopped
2 ounces shallots, chopped
2 cups white mushrooms, chopped
16 large kale leaves, discard hard stem and ribs, finely chopped
6 slices bacon, chopped
1 tablespoon butter, melted
1 cup Parmesan cheese, shredded

**Directions:**

1. In a bowl, add the eggs, milk, salt, and pepper, and beat until well combined.

2. Add bacon to a skillet. Place the skillet over medium heat. Cook until the bacon is crisp.

3. Stir in the green pepper, shallots, and mushrooms. Sauté for 1–2 minutes.

4. Add kale and stir. Turn off the heat.

5. Grease the inside of the Crock Pot with butter. Transfer the vegetable mixture into the pot.

6. Sprinkle with cheese. Add the egg mixture and stir to combine.

7. Close the lid. Set the Crock Pot on Low and cook for 7–8 hours or until set.

**Nutritional Information (Per Serving)**
Calories: 278
Fat: 18 g
Sat Fat: 7.2 g
Carbohydrates: 9.1 g
Fiber: 0.9 g
Sugar: 3 g
Protein: 21.2 g

# Meat and Veggie Casserole

**Servings:** 12
**Cooking Time:** 6 hours
**Ingredients:**
3 cups sweet potatoes, sliced
1 pound breakfast sausage, crumbled
2 cups zucchini squash, sliced
6 green onions, sliced
12 eggs
¼ cup water
Salt and pepper to taste

**Directions:**
1. Heat the sausage in a skillet until brown.
2. Line the bottom of your Crock Pot with a disposable liner.
3. Place the sliced sweet potatoes on the bottom and cover them with the cooked sausage. Add the zucchini and onions.
4. Beat the eggs with the water and add salt and pepper. Pour into the Crock Pot.
5. Cook for 6 hours on the Low setting.

**Nutritional Information (Per Serving)**
Calories: 241
Fat: 15.2 g
Sat Fat: 4.8 g
Carbohydrates: 12.0 g
Fiber: 2 g
Sugar: 1.1 g
Protein: 13.8 g

# Cauliflower Hash Brown Egg Cups

**Servings:** 6
**Cooking Time:** 6 hours
**Ingredients:**
1 head cauliflower, grated to a rice-like texture
¼ cup cheddar cheese or Mozzarella cheese
7 eggs
2 tablespoons Parmesan cheese, grated
Salt and pepper to taste
¼ teaspoon garlic powder

**Directions:**
1. Grease 6 muffin cups with cooking spray.
2. Lightly steam the cauliflower. Squeeze the cauliflower of excess moisture. Add into a bowl. Add 1 egg, cheese, salt, pepper, and garlic powder and mix well.
3. Divide into the 6 muffin cups. Press it into the cups making a well in each cup.
4. Place crumpled aluminum foil at the bottom of the Crock Pot (this step can be avoided if your pot is ceramic). Place the muffin molds inside the pot.
5. Close the lid. Set the pot on High and cook for 4 hours.
6. Open the lid and crack an egg in each muffin cup. Sprinkle with salt and pepper.
7. Cook on High for 2 hours or until the eggs are set.
8. Cool for a while. Run a knife around the edges of the egg cups. Remove them carefully and serve.

**Nutritional Information (Per Serving)**
Calories: 110
Fat: 7.1 g
Sat Fat: 2.9 g
Carbohydrates: 3 g
Fiber: 1.1 g

Sugar: 1.5 g
Protein: 9.1 g

# Nutty Pumpkin Bread

**Servings:** 10
**Cooking Time:** 2 hours
**Ingredients:**
1 cup whole-wheat flour
1 cup all-purpose flour
1 teaspoon baking soda
½ teaspoon ground cinnamon
¼ teaspoon ginger, minced
Pinch of ground nutmeg
Salt to taste
2 eggs
2/3 cup maple syrup
½ cup canola oil
1 tablespoon milk
1 teaspoon vanilla extract
1 cup canned pumpkin puree
½ cup mini dark chocolate chips
½ cup walnuts, chopped

**Directions:**
1. Grease a loaf pan that fits inside a large Crock Pot.
2. In a large bowl, add flours, baking powder, spices, and salt, and mix well.
3. In another bowl, add eggs, maple syrup, oil, milk, and vanilla extract, and beat until well combined. Add pumpkin puree, and beat until well combined.

4. Add the egg mixture into the flour mixture, and mix until well combined.

5. Fold in chocolate chips and walnuts.

6. Transfer the mixture into the prepared loaf pan. Carefully arrange the loaf pan in the Crock Pot.

7. Set the Crock Pot on High. Cover it, and cook for about 2 hours or until a toothpick inserted in the center comes out clean.

8. Remove the loaf pan from the Crock Pot, and place it on a wire rack to cool for about 10 minutes.

9. Carefully invert the bread onto the wire rack, and cool completely before slicing.

**Nutritional Information (Per Serving)**
Calories: 374
Fat: 19.9 g
Sat Fat: 3.5 g
Carbohydrates: 46.9 g
Fiber: 3.2 g
Sugar: 24.5 g
Protein: 6.1 g

# Veggie Omelet

**Servings:** 4
**Cooking Time:** 2 hours
**Ingredients:**
½ cup milk
6 eggs
⅛ teaspoon red chili powder
⅛ teaspoon garlic powder
Salt and pepper to taste
1 medium red bell pepper, seeded and sliced thinly
1 cup broccoli florets
1 small yellow onion, chopped
2 tablespoons fresh parsley, chopped

**Directions:**
1. In a bowl, add milk, eggs, chili powder, garlic powder, salt, and black pepper, and beat until well combined.

2. Lightly grease a Crock Pot. In the bottom of the Crock Pot, mix the bell pepper, broccoli, and onion.

3. Pour egg mixture on top and gently stir to combine.

4. Set the Crock Pot on High. Cover and cook for about 1½–2 hours or until the desired doneness of eggs.

5. Transfer the omelet onto a serving plate. Carefully cut into 4 wedges of equal size.

6. Serve hot with a garnish of parsley.

**Nutritional Information (Per Serving)**
Calories: 135
Fat: 7.4 g
Sat Fat: 2.4 g
Carbohydrates: 7.6 g
Fiber: 1.5 g
Sugar: 4.6 g
Protein: 10.5 g

# Easy Frittata

**Servings:** 8
**Cooking Time:** 8–9 hours
**Ingredients:**
12 large eggs, beaten
1 cup milk
1½ cups artichoke hearts, chopped
½ cup green bell pepper, chopped
Salt and pepper to taste
1 tomato, deseeded, chopped
½ cup green onion, chopped
½ cup cheddar cheese, grated

**Directions:**
1. Spray the bottom of the Crock Pot with cooking spray.
2. Add all the ingredients except cheese into a bowl and mix well. Pour into the Crock Pot.
3. Close the lid. Set the pot on Low and cook for 8–9 hours or until the desired doneness of eggs.
4. Sprinkle cheese on top. Cover and let it sit for a few minutes.
5. Slice into 8 wedges and serve.

**Nutritional Information (Per Serving)**
Calories: 162
Fat: 10.5 g
Sat Fat: 4.2 g
Carbohydrates: 4.8 g
Fiber: 0.7 g
Sugar: 3.1 g
Protein: 12.7 g

# Sweet Sausage and Peppers

**Servings:** 6

**Cooking Time:** 2 hours 10 minutes

**Ingredients:**

12 ounces breakfast sausage, cut into pieces

1 cup red onion, sliced

2 cups mushrooms, sliced

2 cups bell pepper in any color, chopped

1 teaspoon olive oil

¼ cup water

2 teaspoons fresh parsley

2 teaspoons fresh tarragon

**Directions:**

1. Brown your sausage in a skillet for five minutes, and then stir the onion in the same skillet with the olive oil until it starts to soften.

2. Combine the sausage, onion, and mushrooms in the Crock Pot. Pour the water over the top.

3. Cover the Crock Pot, and let it cook on High for an hour.

4. Stir in the bell peppers, and allow it to cook for one more hour.

5. Sprinkle with parsley and tarragon before serving.

**Nutritional Information (Per Serving)**

Calories: 243

Fat: 18.6 g

Sat Fat: 6.3 g

Carbohydrates: 6.3 g

Fiber: 1.2 g

Sugar: 2.0 g

Protein: 12.6 g

Sodium: 736 mg

# Oats, Nuts, and Seeds Granola

**Servings:** 14
**Cooking Time:** 2½ hours
**Ingredients:**

4 cups old-fashioned rolled oats
¼ cup almonds, chopped
¼ cup walnuts, chopped
¼ cup sunflower seeds
¼ cup pumpkin seeds
¼ cup brown sugar
½ teaspoon ground cinnamon
¼ teaspoon salt
½ cup coconut oil
½ cup honey
1 tablespoon vanilla extract
½ cup raisins

**Directions:**

1. Grease a Crock Pot with cooking spray. Add oats, nuts, seeds, brown sugar, cinnamon, and salt, and mix well.

2. In a bowl, add the remaining ingredients except for raisins and mix until well combined.

3. Pour the honey mixture over the oat mixture, and stir to combine well.

4. Set the Crock Pot on High. Cover the Crock Pot partially, and cook for about 2½ hours, stirring every 30 minutes.

5. Turn off the Crock Pot and immediately stir in raisins.

6. Transfer the granola to a large baking sheet, and set it aside at room temperature to cool completely.

7. Serve this granola with milk and your desired topping.

8. You can preserve this granola in an airtight container.

**Nutritional Information (Per Serving)**

Calories: 263
Fat: 13.1 g
Sat Fat: 7.4 g
Carbohydrates: 33.8 g
Fiber: 3.1 g
Sugar: 16 g
Protein: 4.9 g
Sodium: 46 mg

# Vanilla Tapioca Pudding

**Servings:** 8
**Cooking Time:** 6 hours
**Ingredients:**
2 eggs, beaten lightly
4 cups milk
2/3 cup sugar
½ cup small pearl tapioca
1 teaspoon vanilla extract
¼ teaspoon ground cinnamon
½ cup fresh blueberries

**Directions:**
1. In a Crock Pot, add all ingredients except blueberries, and mix until well combined.
2. Set the Crock Pot on Low.
3. Cover and cook for about 6 hours.
4. Serve warm with a topping of blueberries.

**Nutritional Information (Per Serving)**
Calories: 196
Fat: 5.1 g
Sat Fat: 2.9 g
Carbohydrates: 32.2 g

Fiber: 0.3 g
Sugar: 23.3 g
Protein: 6.5 g
Sodium: 76 mg

# Spinach Quiche

**Servings:** 4
**Cooking Time:** 4 hours
**Ingredients:**
10 ounces frozen chopped spinach, thawed and squeezed
4 ounces feta cheese, shredded
2 cups milk
4 eggs
¼ teaspoon red pepper flakes, crushed
Salt and pepper to taste

**Directions:**
1. In a Crock Pot, add all ingredients, and mix until well combined.
2. Set the Crock Pot on Low. Cover and cook for about 4 hours.

**Nutritional Information (Per Serving)**
Calories: 215
Fat: 13.2 g
Sat Fat: 7.1 g
Carbohydrates: 10.1 g
Fiber: 1.6 g
Sugar: 7.3 g
Protein: 15.6 g

# Apple Pie Quinoa Porridge

**Servings:** 5
**Cooking Time:** 8 hours
**Ingredients:**
*For Porridge:*
1 cup uncooked quinoa, rinsed under cold water
1 apple, cored and chopped
3 tablespoons flax meal
3½ cups unsweetened soy milk
2 tablespoons pure maple syrup
1 tablespoon coconut oil, melted
1 teaspoon vanilla extract
1 teaspoon ground cinnamon
⅛ teaspoon ginger, minced
Pinch of ground cloves
Pinch of ground cardamom
Pinch of ground nutmeg
Salt to taste

*For Topping:*
1 apple, cored and sliced
3 tablespoons dried cranberries
3 tablespoons pecans, chopped

**Directions:**
1. Lightly grease the Crock Pot with nonstick cooking spray. Add quinoa, chopped apple, flax meal, soy milk, maple syrup, coconut oil, vanilla extract, spices, and salt, and stir to combine well.

2. Set the Crock Pot on Low. Cover and cook for about 8 hours.

3. Transfer the quinoa porridge to serving bowls.

4. Top with chopped apple, cranberries, and pecans.

5. If you like a creamier texture, pour in more milk while serving.

**Nutritional Information (Per Serving)**
Calories: 386
Fat: 14.3 g
Sat Fat: 3.6 g
Carbohydrates: 53.5 g
Fiber: 7.9 g
Sugar: 21.5 g
Protein: 12.2 g

# Cheesy Grits

**Servings:** 8

**Cooking Time:** 8 hours 10 minutes

**Ingredients:**

1½ cups hand-ground grits

6 cups water

1 teaspoon salt

5 tablespoons butter

½ cup shredded Cheddar cheese; sharp Cheddar is great

Pepper to taste

**Directions:**

1. Lightly grease the inside of a Crock Pot, or coat with a nonstick spray.

2. Mix together the grits, water, and salt, and pour it into the Crock Pot.

3. Cook for 8 hours on Low.

4. Open the pot, and spoon in the butter in separate pieces.

5. Stir hard to combine the grits with the butter.

6. Add the shredded cheese and pepper.

**Nutritional Information (Per Serving)**

Calories: 201

Fat: 9.9 g

Sat Fat: 6.1 g

Carbohydrates: 23.4 g

Fiber: 0.5 g

Sugar: 0.2 g

Protein: 4.4 g

Sodium: 341 mg

# Chocolate Oatmeal

**Servings:** 4
**Cooking Time:** 3 hours
**Ingredients:**
4 cups water
½ cup unsweetened coconut milk
1 tablespoon cocoa powder
1 tablespoon maple syrup
1 teaspoon vanilla extract
¼ teaspoon salt
1 cup steel-cut oats
1 banana, peeled and sliced

**Directions:**
1. Lightly grease the Crock Pot with nonstick cooking spray.
2. In a large bowl, mix all ingredients except oats.
3. Spread oats in the bottom of the Crock Pot. Pour milk mixture evenly over oats.
4. Set the Crock Pot on High. Cover and cook for about 3 hours.
5. Serve hot with a topping of banana slices.

**Nutritional Information (Per Serving)**
Calories: 192
Fat: 8.8 g
Sat Fat: 6.7 g
Carbohydrates: 26.5 g
Fiber: 3.9 g
Sugar: 7.9 g
Protein: 3.9 g
Sodium: 307 mg

# Broccoli Chop Breakfast

**Servings:** 8
**Cooking Time:** 2–4 hours
**Ingredients:**
5 cups broccoli, chopped
12 ounces breakfast sausage, chopped
10 eggs
½ cup water
2 cloves garlic, sliced
Salt and pepper to taste

**Directions:**
1. Cook sausage in a skillet until brown.
2. Line your Crock Pot with a disposable liner and place half the broccoli on the bottom.
3. Put half the sausage on top of the broccoli and then add the rest of the broccoli and then the sausage, so it's layered.
4. Whisk together the eggs, garlic, water, salt, and pepper until combined and pour over the ingredients in the pot.
5. Cook on High for 2 hours or Low for 4 hours.

**Nutritional Information (Per Serving)**
Calories: 243
Fat: 17.7 g
Sat Fat: 5.6 g
Carbohydrates: 4.5 g
Fiber: 1.5 g
Sugar: 1.4 g
Protein: 16.8 g

# CHAPTER THREE
# Vegetables and Beans

## Vegetable Curry

**Servings:** 4
**Cooking Time:** 4 hours 40 minutes
**Ingredients:**
1 green bell pepper, seeded and chopped
1 red bell pepper, seeded and chopped
2 sweet potatoes, peeled and cubed
1 cup carrot, peeled and chopped
1 (14 oz.) can coconut cream
2 tablespoons curry powder
2 tablespoons all-purpose flour
Salt and pepper to taste
1 cup fresh green peas, shelled
¼ cup fresh cilantro, chopped

**Directions:**
1. In a Crock Pot, add all ingredients except peas and cilantro, and mix well.
2. Set the Crock Pot on High. Cover and cook for about 3–4 hours.
3. Uncover the Crock Pot, add peas, and stir well.
4. Cover and cook for another 30–40 minutes.
5. Serve with a garnish of cilantro.

**Nutritional Information (Per Serving)**
Calories: 401
Fat: 24.6 g
Sat Fat: 21.1 g

Carbohydrates: 43.7 g
Fiber: 9.8 g
Sugar: 10.2 g
Protein: 2 g

# Quinoa and Beans Chili

**Servings:** 8
**Cooking Time:** 3½ hours
**Ingredients:**
1 (15 oz.) can red kidney beans, rinsed and drained
1 (15 oz.) can black beans, rinsed and drained
½ cup uncooked quinoa, rinsed
2 ounces canned chopped green chilies
1 (14 oz.) can diced tomatoes with juice
1 chipotle chili in adobo sauce, chopped
1 small onion, chopped
2 garlic cloves, minced
3 cups vegetable broth
1 tablespoon red chili powder
½ tablespoon ground cumin
½ teaspoon sugar
Salt and pepper to taste
2 tablespoons fresh lime juice
3 scallions, chopped

**Directions:**
1. In a large Crock Pot, add all ingredients except scallions, and mix well.

2. Set the Crock Pot on High. Cover and cook for about 3–3½ hours.

3. Garnish with scallion and serve.

**Nutritional Information (Per Serving)**
Calories: 461
Fat: 3.2 g
Sat Fat: 0.6 g
Carbohydrates: 83 g
Fiber: 20.3 g
Sugar: 7.9 g

Protein: 8.5 g

# Stuffed Mushrooms

**Servings:** 4
**Cooking Time:** 3 hours
**Ingredients:**
1 pound mushrooms
½ cup chicken broth
6 ounces Boursin cheese
Paprika to garnish

**Directions:**
1. Remove the stems from the mushrooms, and reserve them for another use.

2. Fill all the mushrooms with Boursin cheese, and place them at the bottom of the Crock Pot.

3. Pour some chicken broth around the mushrooms to fill the bottom of the pot. Sprinkle with paprika.

4. Close the lid. Set the pot on High and cook for 2–3 hours.

5. Serve hot.

**Nutritional Information (Per Serving)**
Calories: 199
Fat: 18.9 g
Sat Fat: 12.8 g
Carbohydrates: 5.2 g
Fiber: 1.1 g
Sugar: 3.4 g
Protein: 7 g
Sodium: 357 mg

# Potato, Pumpkin, and Beans Soup

**Servings:** 6
**Cooking Time:** 8 hours
**Ingredients:**
1 tablespoon vegetable oil
1 onion, chopped
1 potato, scrubbed and cubed
1 (15 oz.) can Great Northern Beans, rinsed and drained
¾ cup pumpkin puree
1 cup tomato puree
3 cups vegetable broth
¼ cup coconut milk
1 teaspoon dried rosemary, crushed
1 teaspoon ground cumin
½ teaspoon red pepper flakes, crushed
½ teaspoon paprika
Salt and pepper to taste
2 tablespoons fresh lime juice
¼ cup fresh cilantro leaves, chopped

**Directions:**
1. In a large Crock Pot, add all ingredients except cilantro leaves, and mix well.

2. Set the Crock Pot on Low. Cover and cook for about 6–8 hours.

3. Serve hot with a garnish of cilantro leaves.

**Nutritional Information (Per Serving)**
Calories: 384
Fat: 6.5 g
Sat Fat: 3 g
Carbohydrates: 63.9 g
Fiber: 17.2 g
Sugar: 7.2 g

Protein: 20.4 g

# Potato Salad

**Servings:** 8
**Cooking Time:** 6 hours
**Ingredients:**
2 pounds red potatoes, peeled and sliced
1 teaspoon olive oil
1 cup celery, chopped
1 cup onion, chopped
½ cup green bell pepper, seeded and chopped
½ cup balsamic vinegar
¼ cup olive oil
3 tablespoons whole-grain mustard
6 cooked bacon slices, chopped
¼ cup fresh parsley, chopped

**Directions:**
1. In a Crock Pot, mix all ingredients except bacon and parsley.
2. Set the Crock Pot on Low. Cover and cook for about 5–6 hours.
3. Top with bacon and parsley, and serve immediately.

**Nutritional Information (Per Serving)**
Calories: 267
Fat: 16.1 g
Sat Fat: 3.9 g
Carbohydrates: 20.7 g
Fiber: 2.5 g
Sugar: 2 g
Protein: 10.2 g
Sodium: 530 mg

# Broccoli Cauliflower "Rice"

**Servings:** 8

**Cooking Time:** 2–3 hours

**Ingredients:**

1 pound cauliflower, grated

8 ounces broccoli, chopped

4–5 tablespoons water

4 tablespoons butter

1 tablespoon lemon zest, grated

2 cloves garlic, minced

½ teaspoon garlic salt or salt

¼ cup Parmesan cheese, grated

Pepper to taste

1 medium onion, minced

**Directions:**

1. Add cauliflower and broccoli into the Crock Pot. Sprinkle water over it.

2. Close the lid. Set the pot on High and cook for about 2–3 hours.

3. Add the rest of the ingredients and stir. Cover and set aside for a while for the flavors to set in.

4. Serve warm.

**Nutritional Information (Per Serving)**

Calories: 91

Fat: 6.5 g

Sat Fat: 4.1 g

Carbohydrates: 6.8 g

Fiber: 2.5 g

Sugar: 2.5 g

Protein: 3.1 g

Sodium: 94 mg

# Squash and Lentil Stew

**Servings:** 6

**Cooking Time:** 6–8 hours

**Ingredients:**

1 large butternut squash, peeled and cubed

1 carrot, peeled and chopped

3 celery stalks, chopped

1 small onion, chopped

1 cup dried red lentils

½ teaspoon dried rosemary, crushed

Salt and pepper to taste

6 cups vegetable broth

¼ cup fresh parsley leaves, chopped

**Directions:**

1. In a Crock Pot, add all ingredients except parsley, and mix well.

2. Set the Crock Pot on Low. Cover and cook for 6–8 hours.

3. Top with parsley, and serve hot.

**Nutritional Information (Per Serving)**

Calories: 282

Fat: 2 g

Sat Fat: 9.5 g

Carbohydrates: 53.6 g

Fiber: 15.8 g

Sugar: 8.3 g

Protein: 16.1 g

# Squash with Apples and Cranberries

**Servings:** 6
**Cooking Time:** 4 hours
**Ingredients:**
1 (3 lb.) butternut squash, peeled, seeded, and cut into cubes
3 apples, peeled, cored, and chopped
½ cup dried cranberries
½ white onion, chopped
1 tablespoon ground cinnamon
1 teaspoon ground nutmeg
Salt and pepper to taste

**Directions:**
1. In a large Crock Pot, add all ingredients and mix well.
2. Set the Crock Pot on High.
3. Cover and cook for about 4 hours.

**Nutritional Information (Per Serving)**
Calories: 173
Fat: 0.6 g
Sat Fat: 0 g
Carbohydrates: 44.7 g
Fiber: 8.5 g
Sugar: 17.4 g
Protein: 2.7 g

# Cheesy Cauliflower Puree

**Servings:** 8
**Cooking Time:** 3 hours
**Ingredients:**
4 cups cauliflower florets
½ cup chicken broth
2 tablespoons butter
Salt and pepper to taste
4 ounces sharp cheese
¼ cup heavy cream

**Directions:**
1. Add all of the ingredients into the Crock Pot.
2. Close the lid. Set the pot on High and cook for 3 hours.
3. Blend with an immersion blender until smooth.
4. Serve warm.

**Nutritional Information (Per Serving)**
Calories: 108
Fat: 8.9 g
Sat Fat: 5.7 g
Carbohydrates: 3.3 g
Fiber: 1.3 g
Sugar: 1.2 g
Protein: 4.9 g

# Eggplant and Tomato Sauce Paste

**Servings:** 6
**Cooking Time:** 7 hours
**Ingredients:**
1 medium eggplant, cut into ½" cubes
1 onion, chopped finely
4 garlic cloves, minced
2 (14 oz.) cans diced tomatoes, drained
1 (6 oz.) can tomato paste
½ cup red wine
2 teaspoons dried oregano, crushed
Salt and pepper to taste
1 pound uncooked penne pasta
¼ cup fresh parsley, chopped

**Directions:**
1. In a Crock Pot, add all ingredients except pasta and parsley.
2. Set the Crock Pot on Low. Cover and cook for about 5–7 hours.
3. In a pan of lightly salted boiling water, cook the pasta for about 8–10 minutes or according to the package's directions. Drain well and set aside.
4. Uncover the Crock Pot, and add pasta and gently stir to combine.
5. Serve immediately with a topping of parsley.

**Nutritional Information (Per Serving)**
Calories: 313
Fat: 2.4 g
Sat Fat: 0 g
Carbohydrates: 59.8 g
Fiber: 6.2 g
Sugar: 10.2 g
Protein: 12.2 g

# Garlic Mushrooms

**Servings:** 3
**Cooking Time:** 3 hours
**Ingredients:**
1 pound white button mushrooms, quartered
3 garlic cloves, minced
¼ cup fresh parsley, chopped
Salt and pepper to taste
2 tablespoons butter, melted
1 teaspoon fresh lemon zest, grated finely

**Directions:**
1. In a Crock Pot, add all ingredients except lemon zest and butter, and mix well.
2. Set the slow cooker on High.
3. Cover and cook for about 2–3 hours.
4. Uncover the Crock Pot, and drizzle with the melted butter.
5. Serve with a topping of lemon zest.

**Nutritional Information (Per Serving)**
Calories: 107
Fat: 8.2 g
Sat Fat: 4.9 g
Carbohydrates: 6.4 g
Fiber: 1.8 g
Sugar: 2.7 g
Protein: 5.2 g

# Veggies with Quinoa and Beans

**Servings:** 5

**Cooking Time:** 6 hours

**Ingredients:**

1¼ cups uncooked quinoa, rinsed under cold water

1¼ cups canned black beans, rinsed and drained

1 cup fresh green beans, trimmed and chopped

1 small carrot, peeled and chopped

1 small orange bell pepper, seeded and chopped

1 small yellow bell pepper, seeded and chopped

1 small onion, chopped

2 garlic cloves, minced

3½ cups vegetable broth

Salt and pepper to taste

2 tablespoons fresh cilantro leaves, chopped

**Directions:**

1. In a Crock Pot, mix all ingredients except cilantro, and stir to combine.

2. Set the Crock Pot on Low. Cover and cook for about 4–6 hours.

3. Uncover the Crock Pot, and with a fork, fluff the quinoa mixture.

4. Serve with a topping of cilantro.

**Nutritional Information (Per Serving)**

Calories: 382

Fat: 4.4 g

Sat Fat: 0.8 g

Carbohydrates: 66 g

Fiber: 12.3 g

Sugar: 5.3 g

Protein: 21.1 g

# Creamy Broccoli Soup

**Servings:** 6
**Cooking Time:** 4 hours
**Ingredients:**
1 medium onion, sliced
1 carrot, peeled and chopped
3 cups broccoli, chopped
2 garlic cloves, minced
¼ teaspoon cayenne pepper
1 teaspoon lemon juice
2 teaspoons all-purpose flour
½ teaspoon dried oregano, crushed
Salt and pepper to taste
4 cups chicken broth
1 cup heavy cream

**Directions:**
1. In a Crock Pot, add all ingredients except cream, and mix until well combined.
2. Set the Crock Pot on Low. Cover and cook for about 3–4 hours.
3. Uncover and immediately add cream, and stir until well combined.
4. Serve hot.

**Nutritional Information (Per Serving)**
Calories: 127
Fat: 8.5 g
Sat Fat: 4.9 g
Carbohydrates: 8 g
Fiber: 1.9 g
Sugar: 2.6 g
Protein: 5.4 g
Sodium: 540 mg

# Zucchini Gratin

**Servings:** 4
**Cooking Time:** 3 hours
**Ingredients:**
2 cups zucchini slices
Salt and pepper to taste
1 tablespoon butter, melted
¼ cup heavy whipping cream
½ small onion, thinly sliced
¾ cup pepper Jack cheese, shredded
¼ teaspoon garlic powder

**Directions:**
1. Grease the inside of the Crock Pot with a bit of oil.
2. Place onion slices at the bottom of the pot. Layer with zucchini slices followed by cheese.
3. Mix the rest of the ingredients in a bowl and pour over the cheese layer.
4. Close the lid. Set the pot on High and cook for 2–3 hours or until zucchini is tender.
5. Let it sit for a while before serving. Slice into 4 equal portions and serve.

**Nutritional Information (Per Serving)**
Calories: 131
Fat: 11.2 g
Sat Fat: 7.2 g
Carbohydrates: 3.2 g
Fiber: 0.9 g
Sugar: 1.5 g
Protein: 5.3 g

# Coconut Creamed Spinach

**Servings:** 4
**Cooking Time:** 2–3 hours
**Ingredients:**
½ cup coconut milk
¼ teaspoon ground nutmeg
¼ teaspoon cayenne pepper
8 cups baby spinach
Salt to taste

**Directions:**
1. Add all the ingredients into the Crock Pot.
2. Close the lid. Set the pot on Low and cook for 2–3 hours.
3. Stir and serve.

**Nutritional Information (Per Serving)**
Calories: 84
Fat: 7.5 g
Sat Fat: 6.4 g
Carbohydrates: 4 g
Fiber: 2 g
Sugar: 1.3 g
Protein: 2.4 g

# Italian Zucchini and Yellow Squash

**Servings:** 3
**Cooking Time:** 5–6 hours
**Ingredients:**
1 medium yellow squash, quartered, sliced
1 medium zucchini, quartered, sliced
1 teaspoon Italian seasoning or to taste
¼ teaspoon sea salt
2 tablespoons Parmesan cheese, grated
Pepper to taste
½ teaspoon garlic powder
2 tablespoons cold butter, cubed

**Directions:**
1. Add squash and zucchini into the Crock Pot.
2. Sprinkle with salt, garlic powder, pepper, and Italian seasoning.
3. Place butter cubes all over the vegetables. Sprinkle cheese on top.
4. Close the lid. Set the pot on Low and cook for 5–6 hours or until tender.
5. Stir and serve.

**Nutritional Information (Per Serving)**
Calories: 107
Fat: 9.2 g
Sat Fat: 5.5 g
Carbohydrates: 5 g
Fiber: 1.5 g
Sugar: 2.5 g
Protein: 3 g
Sodium: 259 mg

# CHAPTER FOUR

# Poultry

## Chicken Broccoli

**Servings:** 4
**Cooking Time:** 5 hours
**Ingredients:**
1 pound skinless, boneless chicken thighs, cubed
1½ cups coconut milk
1 small white onion, chopped
2 garlic cloves, minced
2 cups broccoli, chopped
Salt and pepper to taste
1 tablespoon fresh lemon juice

**Directions:**
1. In a Crock Pot, add all ingredients except lemon juice, and mix well.
2. Set the Crock Pot on Low. Cover and cook for about 4–5 hours.
3. Serve hot with a drizzling of lemon juice.

**Nutritional Information (Per Serving)**
Calories: 187
Fat: 6.5 g
Sat Fat: 3.0 g
Carbohydrates: 7.3 g
Fiber: 1.7 g
Sugar: 2.4 g
Protein: 24.3 g

# Ranch Chicken

**Servings:** 3
**Cooking Time:** 4 hours 45 minutes
**Ingredients:**
*For ranch seasoning mix:*
½ tablespoon dried parsley
¾ teaspoon dried dill
¼ teaspoon dried onion
¼ teaspoon salt
1 teaspoon dried chives
¼ teaspoon paprika
¼ teaspoon garlic powder
Freshly ground pepper to taste

*For ranch chicken:*
3 chicken breast halves, skinless and boneless
¾ teaspoon steak seasoning
2 teaspoons ranch seasoning mix (given above)
½ cup chicken broth
2 small shallots, sliced
6 slices bacon
3 cups broccoli florets
¼ cup mayonnaise
Salt to taste
1½ tablespoons red wine vinegar

**Directions:**
1. Mix all the ingredients of ranch seasoning in a small jar. Use 2 teaspoons of it.

2. Place chicken in the Crock Pot. Season the chicken with ranch seasoning and steak seasoning. Add the broth and place shallots on top.

3. Close the lid. Set the pot on Low and cook for 4 hours.

4. Add broccoli and cook for 45 minutes.

5. Meanwhile, cook the bacon in a skillet until crisp. Crumble the bacon when cooled.

6. When the chicken is done, shred it and add it back into the pot. Add vinegar, salt, bacon, and mayonnaise and mix well.

7. Serve warm.

**Nutritional Information (Per Serving)**
Calories: 442
Fat: 25.5 g
Sat Fat: 6.2 g
Carbohydrates: 13.1 g
Fiber: 2.5 g
Sugar: 3.1 g
Protein: 39.1 g

# Chicken Stew

**Servings:** 2
**Cooking Time:** 6–8 hours
**Ingredients:**
1 cup chicken stock
2 cups chicken, skinless, boneless, chopped into chunks
1 stalk celery, chopped
3 cloves garlic, minced
¼ cup onion, chopped
¼ teaspoon dried rosemary
¼ teaspoon dried oregano
¼ teaspoon dried thyme
1 tablespoon olive oil
½ cup fresh spinach, chopped
Salt and pepper to taste
½ cup heavy cream

⅛ teaspoon xanthan gum

**Directions:**

1. Add celery, chicken, stock, garlic, onion, herbs, and olive oil into the Crock Pot and stir.

2. Close the lid, set the pot on Low, and cook for 6–8 hours.

3. Add spinach, salt, pepper, and cream.

4. Sprinkle some xanthan gum to get the desired thickness. Whisk well.

5. Heat thoroughly. Ladle into bowls and serve.

**Nutritional Information (Per Serving)**
Calories: 397
Fat: 22.7 g
Sat Fat: 9.2 g
Carbohydrates: 4.9 g
Fiber: 1.4 g
Sugar: 1.2 g
Protein: 42.3 g
Sodium: 530 mg

# Honey-Glazed Chicken

**Servings:** 6
**Cooking Time:** 8 hours
**Ingredients:**
2¼ pounds chicken pieces
1 medium onion, chopped
⅓ cup chives, minced
1½ tablespoons ginger, minced
3 tablespoons sherry
2½ tablespoons honey
1½ tablespoons soy sauce
2 tablespoons black sesame seeds, toasted

**Directions:**
1. In the bottom of a Crock Pot, place chicken pieces.
2. In a bowl, add remaining ingredients except for sesame seeds, and mix well. Pour the mixture evenly over the chicken.
4. Set the Crock Pot on Low. Cover and cook for about 6–8 hours.
6. Serve hot with a garnish of sesame seeds.

**Nutritional Information (Per Serving)**
Calories: 391
Fat: 14.2 g
Sat Fat: 3.7 g
Carbohydrates: 11.1 g
Fiber: 1 g
Sugar: 8.2 g
Protein: 50.4 g
Sodium: 374 mg

# Roasted Whole Chicken

**Servings:** 6
**Cooking Time:** 8 hours
**Ingredients:**
1 (3½ lb.) whole chicken, cleaned, pat dried
5 garlic cloves, peeled
1 large carrot, peeled and chopped
1 large celery stalk, chopped
1 medium onion, chopped
1 tablespoon Herbs de Provence
Salt and pepper to taste
3 tablespoons fresh lemon juice

**Directions:**
1. Stuff the chicken cavity with garlic cloves.
2. Sprinkle the chicken all over with salt, pepper, and Herbs de Provence.
3. In the bottom of a Crock Pot, place the vegetables.
4. Arrange the chicken over the vegetables. Drizzle with lemon juice.
5. Set the Crock Pot on Low. Cover and cook for about 6–8 hours.
6. Serve with fresh baby greens.

**Nutritional Information (Per Serving)**
Calories: 520
Fat: 19.7 g
Sat Fat: 5.5 g
Carbohydrates: 3.7 g
Fiber: 0.8 g
Sugar: 1.5 g
Protein: 77.1 g

# Asian Chicken

**Servings:** 6

**Cooking Time:** 6 hours

**Ingredients:**

12 ounces chicken pieces (thighs work best)

1 cup shredded carrots

½ cup green onions, chopped

1 pound cabbage, shredded

5 cloves garlic, minced

1 tablespoon soy sauce

4 teaspoons sesame oil

2 tablespoons water

1 teaspoon white vinegar

1 teaspoon honey

1 tablespoon grated ginger

**Directions:**

1. Combine the ginger, honey, vinegar, water, sesame oil, garlic, and soy sauce in a small bowl.

2. Put the cabbage, onions, and carrots into the Crock Pot and combine.

3. Place the chicken on top of the cabbage and drizzle with the mixture from the bowl.

4. Cook on low for 6 hours.

**Nutritional Information (Per Serving)**

Calories: 176

Fat: 7.4 g

Sat Fat: 1.6 g

Carbohydrates: 9.4 g

Fiber: 2.7 g

Sugar: 4.6 g

Protein: 18.1 g

Sodium: 228 mg

# Chicken Tortillas

**Servings:** 4
**Cooking Time:** 8 hours
**Ingredients:**
*For Chicken:*
1 cup chicken broth
1 (1¼ oz.) package dry taco seasoning mix
1 pound skinless, boneless chicken breasts

*For Tortillas:*
8 corn tortillas, warmed
1 cup purple cabbage, shredded
1 cup carrot, peeled and shredded
½ cup sour cream

**Directions:**
1. In a bowl, mix broth and taco seasoning.
2. In the Crock Pot, place chicken breasts and top with broth mixture.
3. Set the Crock Pot on Low. Cover and cook for about 6–8 hours.
4. Uncover the Crock Pot, and with 2 forks, shred the chicken breasts. Mix completely with pan juices.
5. Divide the shredded chicken between warm tortillas. Top with cabbage, carrot, and sour cream and serve.

**Nutritional Information (Per Serving)**
Calories: 361
Fat: 11.8 g
Sat Fat: 5.6 g
Carbohydrates: 32.3 g
Fiber: 4.1 g
Sugar: 2.5 g
Protein: 30.6 g

Sodium: 799 mg

# Chicken and Beans Salad

**Servings:** 8
**Cooking Time:** 5 hours
**Ingredients:**
*For Chicken:*
2 (8 oz.) skinless, boneless chicken breasts
2 tablespoons taco seasoning
2 cups canned black beans, rinsed and drained
2 cups chunky salsa

*For Dressing:*
1 cup buttermilk
1 large avocado, peeled, pitted, and chopped roughly
1 jalapeño, seeded and chopped
3 tablespoons scallions, chopped
3 tablespoons fresh cilantro, chopped
1 tablespoon lime juice
⅛ teaspoon ground cumin
Salt and pepper to taste

*For Salad:*
8 cups romaine lettuce, chopped
⅓ cup cheddar cheese, shredded
½ cup scallions, chopped

**Directions:**
1. Season chicken evenly with taco seasoning.
2. In a Crock Pot, place chicken, followed by beans and salsa.

3. Set the Crock Pot on Low. Cover and cook for about 4–5 hours.

4. Uncover the Crock Pot, and transfer the chicken into a bowl. Set aside to cool slightly.

5. Chop the chicken into bite-sized pieces. Return the chicken to the Crock Pot, and mix with beans and salsa.

6. For the dressing, in a blender, add all ingredients and pulse until smooth.

7. Divide lettuce onto serving plates. Top with the chicken mixture, followed by the cheese and dressing.

8. Serve immediately with a garnish of scallions.

**Nutritional Information (Per Serving)**
Calories: 470
Fat: 13.4 g
Sat Fat: 4.5 g
Carbohydrates: 54.4 g
Fiber: 14.3 g
Sugar: 6.8 g
Protein: 36.8 g
Sodium: 653 mg

# Citrus Chicken

**Servings:** 6
**Cooking Time:** 4 hours
**Ingredients:**
3 pounds chicken
2 limes, juiced
1 lemon, juiced
1 orange, juiced
4 tablespoons fresh cilantro
3 tomatoes, chopped
1 red onion, chopped
1 teaspoon red pepper flakes
Salt and pepper to taste

**Directions:**
1. Place the chicken at the bottom of the Crock Pot and add the citrus juice, tomatoes, onion, red pepper, and cilantro.

2. Stir everything together and cook on High for 4 hours. The chicken will be tender and easily shredded, and you'll love the tangy flavor.

**Nutritional Information (Per Serving)**
Calories: 287
Fat: 5.9 g
Sat Fat: 0 g
Carbohydrates: 7.7 g
Fiber: 1.4 g
Sugar: 4.8 g
Protein: 48.5 g

# Pesto Chicken

**Servings:** 3
**Cooking Time:** 4 hours
**Ingredients:**
2 cups spinach, chopped
1 cup fresh basil leaves, chopped
½ cup walnuts
2 tablespoons olive oil
½ lemon, juiced
1 tablespoon parmesan cheese
¼ cup pine nuts
1 pound cooked chicken, shredded or cubed
2 garlic cloves
½ white onion, sliced
½ cup sundried tomatoes
1 cup chicken broth
Salt and pepper to taste

**Directions:**
1. In a small bowl, mix the spinach, basil, walnuts, olive oil, and lemon juice until paste-like texture.
2. Place the chicken in your Crock Pot and cover with the pesto mix you just prepared.
3. Add the cheese, pine nuts, garlic, onion, and tomatoes.
4. Season with salt and pepper and then cover with the chicken broth.
5. Cook on Low for 4 hours.

**Nutritional Information (Per Serving)**
Calories: 574
Fat: 35.3 g
Sat Fat: 4.3 g
Carbohydrates: 12.9 g
Fiber: 4 g

Sugar: 6.1 g
Protein: 55.1 g

# Salsa Chicken

**Servings:** 4
**Cooking Time:** 6 hours
**Ingredients:**
4 skinless chicken breasts
16 ounces mild salsa
1½ teaspoons dried parsley
½ teaspoon dried cilantro
1 teaspoon onion powder
½ teaspoon paprika
1 teaspoon garlic powder
¼ teaspoon black pepper
2 tablespoons water

**Directions:**
1. Put the chicken pieces at the bottom of your Crock Pot.
2. Add the spices, salsa, and water, and mix well.
3. Cook on low for 6 hours.

**Nutritional Information (Per Serving)**
Calories: 276
Fat: 3.4 g
Sat Fat: 0 g
Carbohydrates: 6.7 g
Fiber: 0.6 g
Sugar: 3.8 g
Protein: 53.6 g
Sodium: 827 mg

# Orange Sauce Meatballs

**Servings:** 6
**Cooking Time:** 5 hours
**Ingredients:**
*For Meatballs:*
1 pound ground turkey
1 egg
2 teaspoons paprika
1 teaspoon ginger, minced
1 teaspoon ground cumin
1 teaspoon cayenne pepper
Salt and pepper to taste

*For Sauce:*
1 cup orange marmalade
¼ cup fresh orange juice
¼ cup chicken broth
1 small jalapeño, seeded and chopped finely
4 scallions, chopped
Salt and pepper to taste

*For Topping:*
2 tablespoons black sesame seeds
¼ cup scallions, chopped

**Directions:**

1. For meatballs, in a large bowl, add all ingredients and mix until well combined.

2. Make small balls of equal size from the turkey mixture.

3. In a Crock Pot, add all sauce ingredients, and mix well. Carefully place the meatballs in the sauce.

4. Set the Crock Pot on Low. Cover and cook for about 4–5 hours.

5. Serve hot with a topping of sesame seeds and scallions.

**Nutritional Information (Per Serving)**
Calories: 352
Fat: 12.5 g
Sat Fat: 3.1 g
Carbohydrates: 39.3 g
Fiber: 1.6 g
Sugar: 33.5 g
Protein: 23.0 g

# Turkey Burritos

**Servings:** 8
**Cooking Time:** 8 hours
**Ingredients:**
1 lb. ground turkey meat
2 tablespoons taco seasoning
1 cup corn kernels, fresh or frozen
1 can drained kidney beans
1 can crushed tomatoes
¾ cup chicken broth
2 cups brown rice
1 cup diced tomatoes
½ cup diced avocados
2 tablespoons chopped cilantro
2 teaspoons lime juice
Salt and pepper to taste
8 flour tortillas
3 cups shredded Cheddar cheese
1 cup sour cream

**Directions:**
1. Break up the turkey meat, and place it in the Crock Pot.
2. Season the meat with taco seasoning.
3. Add in the beans first, then the corn kernels, and, lastly, the crushed tomatoes.
4. Pour in the chicken broth.
5. Cook for 8 hours on low.
6. Stir the ingredients well.
7. Stir in the rice, and stir some more.
8. Cook for another 15 minutes on high.
9. In a bowl, mix the avocado, lime juice, cilantro, salt, and pepper. Set aside.

10. Lay out the corn tortillas on the counter, and fill each with ½ cup turkey filling.

11. Roll up the tortillas, and put them on a baking sheet.

12. Distribute the cheese equally on top of each tortilla.

13. Set the broiler on High, and broil the tortillas for about 5 minutes. Don't let the cheese burn.

14. When serving, add the avocado salsa and sour cream.

**Nutritional Information (Per Serving)**
Calories: 618
Fat: 27.8 g
Sat Fat: 13.5 g
Carbohydrates: 61.7 g
Fiber: 5.5 g
Sugar: 2.8 g
Protein: 30.5 g
Sodium: 902 mg

# Bacon-Wrapped Turkey Breast with Tomatoes

**Servings:** 8
**Cooking Time:** 4 hours
**Ingredients:**
2 pounds turkey breast, chopped
6 tomatoes, peeled and chopped
2 bay leaves
16 ounces bacon slices, thinly cut
¼ teaspoon garlic powder
Salt and pepper to taste

**Directions:**
1. Take the bacon slices and wrap them around the turkey.
2. Add the rest of the ingredients into the Crock Pot and stir.
3. Place the turkey in the pot.
4. Close the lid. Set the pot on High and cook for 4 hours.
5. Discard bay leaves. Slice the turkey and serve with the cooked sauce.

**Nutritional Information (Per Serving)**
Calories: 295
Fat: 16.1 g
Sat Fat: 5.4 g
Carbohydrates: 8.5 g
Fiber: 1.7 g
Sugar: 6.4 g
Protein: 30.2 g

# Slow-Cooked Turkey Breast

**Servings:** 6
**Cooking Time:** 8 hours
**Ingredients:**
2½ pounds bone-in skin-on turkey breast
2 tablespoons olive oil
3 tablespoons Stubbs' chicken spice rub mixture
½ cup chicken broth
Salt and pepper to taste

**Directions:**
1. Sprinkle salt and pepper over the turkey.
2. Place the turkey in the Crock Pot. Rub the olive oil and spice rub over it.
3. Add the broth and close the lid.
4. Set the pot on High and cook for 1 hour and then on Low for 7 hours.

**Nutritional Information (Per Serving)**
Calories: 365
Fat: 14.2 g
Sat Fat: 3.8 g
Carbohydrates: 0.1 g
Fiber: 0 g
Sugar: 0.1 g
Protein: 55.8 g

# Turkey Chili

**Servings:** 6
**Cooking Time:** 7 hours
**Ingredients:**
2 tablespoons olive oil
4 cloves garlic, minced
1 green bell pepper, chopped
1 pound ground turkey
7½ ounces canned diced tomatoes
7½ ounces canned pumpkin puree
1 tablespoon chili powder
½ teaspoon ground cumin
½ teaspoon onion powder
3 ounces tomato paste
¾ cup chicken broth
1 teaspoon ground cinnamon
½ teaspoon sea salt or to taste
Freshly ground pepper to taste

**Directions:**
1. Place a skillet with oil over medium-high heat. Add pepper and garlic. Sauté for a couple of minutes until garlic turns aromatic.
2. Add ground turkey. Sauté until the meat is not pink anymore.
3. Transfer into the Crock Pot.
4. Add the rest of the ingredients and mix well.
5. Close the lid. Set the pot on Low and cook for 7 hours.
6. Ladle into bowls and serve.

**Nutritional Information (Per Serving)**
Calories: 307
Fat: 14.3 g
Sat Fat: 2.4 g
Carbohydrates: 26.3 g
Fiber: 8.4 g

Sugar: 13 g
Protein: 25.8 g
Sodium: 377 mg

# Buffalo Chicken

**Servings:** 3
**Cooking Time:** 7 hours
**Ingredients:**
3 chicken breasts
2 teaspoons ranch seasoning mix
½ cup hot sauce
1 tablespoon butter

**Directions:**
1. Place chicken in the Crock Pot. Drizzle hot sauce over it. Season with ranch seasoning.
2. Close the lid. Set the pot on Low and cook for 6 hours.
3. Remove the chicken with a slotted spoon. Shred the chicken and add it back into the pot.
4. Add butter and cook without the lid on Low for an hour.

**Nutritional Information (Per Serving)**
Calories: 155
Fat: 6.5 g
Sat Fat: 2.5 g
Carbohydrates: 0.7 g
Fiber: 0.1 g
Sugar: 0.5 g
Protein: 21.4 g
Sodium: 1168 mg

# CHAPTER FIVE

# Meats

## Beef Curry

**Servings:** 4
**Cooking Time:** 4 hours
**Ingredients:**
1¼ pounds chuck roast
1 cup water
3 tablespoons coconut milk powder
1½ tablespoons Thai red curry paste
3 pods cardamom, cracked
½ tablespoon dried onion flakes
½ tablespoon ground coriander
A pinch ground nutmeg
1 tablespoon Thai fish sauce
1 tablespoon dried or fresh Thai red chilies
½ tablespoon ground cumin
A pinch ground cloves
½ tablespoon ground ginger

*To serve:*
1 tablespoon coconut milk powder
2 tablespoons cashew, chopped
½ tablespoon Thai red curry paste
A handful fresh cilantro, chopped

**Directions:**
1. Add all the ingredients into the Crock Pot and stir.
2. Close the lid. Set the pot on High and cook for 4 hours.

3. Remove the meat with a slotted spoon and place it in a bowl. Chop or break into smaller pieces.

4. Add all the serving ingredients except cilantro into the Crock Pot and mix.

5. Add the meat back into the pot. Mix well.

6. Garnish with cilantro and serve.

**Nutritional Information (Per Serving)**
Calories: 365
Fat: 17 g
Sat Fat: 7.7 g
Carbohydrates: 5.8 g
Fiber: 0.9 g
Sugar: 1.4 g
Protein: 44.6 g
Sodium: 489 mg

# Beef and Cabbage Stew

**Servings:** 6
**Cooking Time:** 9 hours
**Ingredient:**
2 pounds beef stew meat, trimmed and cubed
Salt and pepper to taste
5 cups green cabbage, chopped
1 large onion, chopped
4 garlic cloves, minced
4 fresh tomatoes, chopped finely
1 cup beef broth
¼ cup fresh parsley, chopped

**Directions:**
1. Season the beef generously with salt and pepper.
2. In the bottom of a large Crock Pot, place the cabbage, onion, and garlic.
3. Top with beef, followed by tomatoes. Pour broth on top, and stir gently to combine.
4. Set the Crock Pot on Low. Cover and cook for about 9 hours.
5. Serve with a garnish of fresh parsley.

**Nutritional Information (Per Serving)**
Calories: 452
Fat: 31.8 g
Sat Fat: 12.6 g
Carbohydrates: 11 g
Fiber: 3.2 g
Sugar: 0 g
Protein: 29.7 g

# Spicy Beef Brisket

**Servings:** 12
**Cooking Time:** 6 hours
**Ingredients:**
1 tablespoon olive oil
1 large white onion, sliced
3 garlic cloves, minced
1 (4 lb.) beef brisket
½ teaspoon red pepper flakes, crushed
½ teaspoon paprika
½ teaspoon ground cumin
¼ teaspoon ground cinnamon
Salt and pepper to taste
½ cup beef broth

**Directions:**
1. In a large Crock Pot, add all ingredients, and mix well.
2. Set the Crock Pot on Low. Cover and cook for about 6 hours.
3. Uncover the Crock Pot, and transfer the brisket onto a cutting board.
4. Set aside for about 10 minutes before slicing.
5. With a sharp knife, cut into desired slices.
6. Serve with a fresh green salad.

**Nutritional Information (Per Serving)**
Calories: 300
Fat: 10.7 g
Sat Fat: 3.8 g
Carbohydrates: 1.6 g
Fiber: 0 g
Sugar: 0.6 g
Protein: 46.3 g

# Miraculous Meatloaf

**Servings:** 6
**Cooking Time:** 6 hours
**Ingredients:**
2 pounds ground beef
3 eggs
2/3 cup shredded coconut
½ onion, minced
1 tablespoon fresh sage
1 teaspoon salt
2 tomatoes, diced
1 teaspoon ground mustard

**Directions:**
1. Place the diced tomatoes in a Crock Pot.
2. Mix all the other ingredients in a large bowl, and shape into a loaf.
3. Place the loaf on top of the tomatoes in the slow cooker.
4. Set the Crock Pot on Low. Cover and cook for 6 hours to ensure no pink is left in the meat.

**Nutritional Information (Per Serving)**
Calories: 573
Fat: 48.5 g
Sat Fat: 22.3 g
Carbohydrates: 5.6 g
Fiber: 1.9 g
Sugar: 0.7 g
Protein: 29.1 g
Sodium: 540 mg

# Italian Meatballs

**Servings:** 4
**Cooking Time:** 6 hours
**Ingredients:**
1 pound ground beef
½ onion, chopped
1 celery stalk, minced
¼ cup parmesan cheese
1 egg
1 teaspoon dried basil
1 teaspoon dried oregano
Salt and pepper to taste
4 tomatoes, chopped
1 can (14 ounces) stewed tomatoes

**Directions:**

1. Make the meatballs by combining beef, onion, celery, cheese, egg, basil, oregano, salt, and pepper. Roll into balls and place on a plate.

2. Pour the stewed tomatoes and fresh tomatoes into the Crock Pot and place meatballs on top.

3. Cook for 6 hours on low heat.

**Nutritional Information (Per Serving)**
Calories: 291
Fat: 9.8 g
Sat Fat: 3.9 g
Carbohydrates: 10.8 g
Fiber: 2.9 g
Sugar: 6.4 g
Protein: 39.4 g

# Hungarian Goulash

**Servings:** 4
**Cooking Time:** 8 hours
**Ingredients:**

1 tablespoon butter
1 tablespoon Hungarian paprika
1 pound beef stew meat, cubed
¼ teaspoon pepper powder or to taste
½ teaspoon salt or to taste
¼ teaspoon caraway seeds
1 bell pepper of any color, chopped
7½ ounces canned diced tomatoes
1 bay leaf
½ cup onion, chopped
1 clove garlic, sliced
1 cup daikon radish, cubed
1 stalk celery, chopped
¾ cup beef broth

**Directions:**

1. Place a skillet with butter over medium heat. When it melts, add onions and sauté until translucent.

2. Add garlic and sauté for a few seconds until fragrant. Add paprika and sauté for 5–8 seconds.

3. Add beef and cook until brown. Add salt, pepper, and caraway seeds and stir. Transfer into the Crock Pot.

4. Add the rest of the ingredients and stir.

5. Close the lid. Set the pot on Low and cook for 8 hours or on High for 4 hours.

6. You can top it with zucchini noodles to complete a meal.

**Nutritional Information (Per Serving)**
Calories: 272

Fat: 10.6 g
Sat Fat: 4.6 g
Carbohydrates: 6.1 g
Fiber: 2.1 g
Sugar: 3.2 g
Protein: 36.3 g
Sodium: 583 mg

# Mississippi Roast

**Servings:** 4
**Cooking Time:** 4 hours
**Ingredients:**
2 pounds beef chuck roast
½ tablespoon dried parsley
½ tablespoon garlic powder
½ tablespoon dried dill
½ tablespoon dried chives
½ tablespoon onion powder
Salt and pepper to taste
8 ounces jarred deli-sliced pepperoncini's, retain the brine
2 tablespoons butter
1 tablespoon better than beef bouillon

**Directions:**
1. Add the meat into the Crock Pot. Place pepperoncini's over it. Pour ½ cup of retained brine into the pot. Add the rest of the ingredients except butter and stir.

2. Place butter on top of the meat.

3. Close the lid. Set the pot on High and cook for 4 hours or until meat comes off the bone.

4. Remove the meat with a slotted spoon and place it in a bowl. Shred with a pair of forks and add it back into the pot.

5. Stir and serve.

**Nutritional Information (Per Serving)**
Calories: 500
Fat: 19.9 g
Sat Fat: 9 g
Carbohydrates: 7.8 g
Fiber: 0.2 g
Sugar: 2.6 g
Protein: 69.9 g

# Braised Short Ribs

**Servings:** 8
**Cooking Time:** 6 hours 10 minutes
**Ingredients:**
5 pounds beef short ribs
1 can beef broth
1 can dark lager beer
1 onion, sliced
¼ cup molasses
2 tablespoons cider vinegar
1 teaspoon hot sauce
1 teaspoon thyme
Salt to taste

**Directions:**
1. Put the short ribs in a Crock Pot.
2. Top the meat with beef broth, molasses, onions, hot sauce, cider vinegar, and thyme.
3. Stir to combine the ingredients.
4. Pour the lager into the Crock Pot.
5. Cook for 6 hours on high or 12 hours on low.
6. Use a tong or slotted spoon to place the ribs on a platter.
7. Transfer the gravy into a bowl.
8. Serve the ribs with gravy and mashed potatoes.

**Nutritional Information (Per Serving)**
Calories: 649
Fat: 26 g
Sat Fat: 9.8 g
Carbohydrates: 10.9 g
Fiber: 0.3 g
Sugar: 6.5 g
Protein: 83.7 g

# Cabbage and Ribs

**Servings:** 4
**Cooking Time:** 6 hours
**Ingredients:**
3 pounds beef short ribs (about six ribs)
1 head of green cabbage, quartered
4 green onions, sliced
4 tablespoons soy sauce
4 tablespoons water
½ cup red wine vinegar
2 cloves garlic, minced
1 tablespoon fresh ginger, grated
½ teaspoon red pepper flakes
1 tablespoon sesame oil

**Directions:**
1. Combine all ingredients in a Crock Pot with the cabbage on top.

2. Cook on High for 6 hours until the meat on the ribs easily pulls away from the bone.

**Nutritional Information (Per Serving)**
Calories: 752
Fat: 46.3 g
Sat Fat: 15.6 g
Carbohydrates: 27 g
Fiber: 5.2 g
Sugar: 11.5 g
Protein: 53.8 g
Sodium: 1077 mg

# Barbecue Beef Stew

**Servings:** 3

**Cooking Time:** 7 hours 30 minutes

**Ingredients:**

*For barbecue sauce:*

3½ ounces tomato paste

½ teaspoon salt

½ teaspoon smoked paprika

6 tablespoons balsamic vinegar

½ teaspoon garlic powder

¼ teaspoon black pepper

*For stew:*

1 pound beef stew meat, boneless, cubed

¼ teaspoon pepper

½ teaspoon arrowroot starch mixed with 1 tablespoon water

½ teaspoon salt

½ tablespoon olive oil

**Directions:**

1. Add all the ingredients of barbecue sauce in a bowl and whisk well.

2. Sprinkle salt and pepper over beef.

3. Place a skillet with oil over medium heat. Add beef and cook until brown on all the sides. Transfer into the Crock Pot.

4. Pour sauce into the pot and mix well.

5. Cover, set the pot on Low, and cook for 7 hours.

6. Add arrowroot starch mixture and stir. Cook on High for 20–30 minutes.

7. Serve warm.

**Nutritional Information (Per Serving)**

Calories: 338

Fat: 12 g
Sat Fat: 3.9 g
Carbohydrates: 7.4 g
Fiber: 1.6 g
Sugar: 4.3 g
Protein: 47.5 g
Sodium: 909 mg

# Slow Cooker Chili

**Servings:** 8
**Cooking Time:** 4 hours
**Ingredients:**
2 pounds lean ground beef
28 ounce can diced tomatoes
1 red bell pepper, chopped
1 green bell pepper, chopped
¼ red onion, chopped
1 jalapeno pepper, seeded and chopped
½ teaspoon cilantro
Salt to taste

**Directions:**
1. In a large skillet, cook the ground beef until brown.
2. Pour it into the Crock Pot and add the tomatoes, peppers, and onion.
3. Sprinkle with cilantro and cook on High for 4 hours.
4. Feel free to add or subtract the amount of jalapeno, depending on how spicy you like your chili. You can lighten it up by using ground turkey instead of ground beef if you want less fat.

**Nutritional Information (Per Serving)**
Calories: 240
Fat: 7.1 g
Sat Fat: 2.7 g
Carbohydrates: 7 g
Fiber: 2.3 g
Sugar: 4.6 g
Protein: 35.6 g

# Herbed Pork with Carrots

**Servings:** 8

**Cooking Time:** 10 hours

**Ingredients:**

2 pounds boneless pork shoulder roast

1 teaspoon dried basil, crushed

1 teaspoon dried oregano, crushed

1 teaspoon dried thyme, crushed

1 tablespoon red pepper flakes, crushed

Salt and pepper to taste

1 large onion, sliced thinly

4 medium carrots, peeled and sliced lengthwise

**Directions:**

1. Rub the pork shoulder generously with dried herbs, salt, and pepper.

2. Arrange the pork in a large bowl, and set aside, covered for at least 3–4 hours.

3. In the bottom of a large Crock Pot, place onion and carrots, and sprinkle with salt and pepper.

4. Place the pork shoulder over the carrots.

5. Set the Crock Pot on Low. Cover and cook for about 8–10 hours.

**Nutritional Information (Per Serving)**

Calories: 354

Fat: 24.4 g

Sat Fat: 8.9 g

Carbohydrates: 5.3 g

Fiber: 1.5 g

Sugar: 2.4 g

Protein: 27 g

# Paprika Pork

**Servings:** 4
**Cooking Time:** 8 hours
**Ingredients:**
1¼ pounds pork tenderloin
2 tablespoons butter, melt
2 cloves garlic, minced
½ tablespoon paprika
½ tablespoon Worcestershire sauce
2 tablespoons chicken broth
A handful fresh thyme, chopped
½ cup onion, chopped
1 small red bell pepper, diced
¼ teaspoon ground caraway
4 teaspoons red wine vinegar
2 tablespoons tomato paste
½ cup sour cream
Salt and pepper to taste

**Directions:**
1. Sprinkle salt and pepper over the pork, brush with butter, and place in the Crock Pot.
2. Add onion, garlic, pepper, and thyme.
3. Add the rest of the ingredients except sour cream into a bowl. Mix well and pour over the pork.
4. Close the lid. Set the pot on Low and cook for 8 hours.
5. Remove the pork with a slotted spoon and place it on your cutting board. When cool enough to handle, shred the pork with a pair of forks.
6. Add the pork back into the pot. Stir well.
7. Cook for 10 minutes without the lid.
8. Add sour cream. Stir and serve.

**Nutritional Information (Per Serving)**
Calories: 347
Fat: 17.1 g
Sat Fat: 9.2 g
Carbohydrates: 7.9 g
Fiber: 1.5 g
Sugar: 3.7 g
Protein: 39.5 g

# Doughless Pizza

**Servings:** 8
**Cooking Time:** 4 hours
**Ingredients:**
1 28-ounce can whole tomatoes
1 6-ounce can tomato paste
1 pound Italian sausage
½ stick pepperoni, sliced
1 cup black olives
1 red onion, sliced
1 cup mushrooms, chopped
1 green bell pepper, chopped
3 cloves garlic, minced
½ cup water
4 sprigs thyme, chopped
6 fresh basil leaves, chopped

**Directions:**
1. Remove sausage from casing, and cook in a skillet until brown.

2. Place the sausage and all the other ingredients into the Crock Pot, and stir until everything is combined.

3. Cook on High for 4 hours.

4. Feel free to customize this recipe to add all your favorite pizza toppings.

**Nutritional Information (Per Serving)**
Calories: 569
Fat: 51.3 g
Sat Fat: 12.4 g
Carbohydrates: 12.0 g
Fiber: 2.8 g
Sugar: 5.4 g
Protein: 16.7 g
Sodium: 1,311 mg

# Pork Burgers

**Servings:** 12
**Cooking Time:** 10 hours
**Ingredients:**
*For Pork:*
1 teaspoon dried oregano, crushed
1 teaspoon ground cumin
½ teaspoon ground coriander
½ teaspoon garlic powder
¼ teaspoon ground cinnamon
Salt and pepper to taste
1 (4 lb.) boneless pork shoulder roast
2 bay leaves
2 cups chicken broth

*For Burgers:*
12 whole-wheat hamburger buns, split
1 cup ketchup
2 cups lettuce, shredded
12 tomato slices
1 onion, sliced

**Directions:**
1. In a bowl, mix oregano, spices, salt, and pepper.
2. Rub the pork roast generously with the spice mixture.
3. In the bottom of a Crock Pot, place bay leaves and top with pork roast. Pour broth on top.
4. Set the Crock Pot on Low. Cover and cook for about 5 hours.
5. Uncover the Crock Pot, and flip over the pork roast. Cover and cook for about another 5 hours.
6. Uncover the Crock Pot, and with 2 forks, shred the pork roast.
7. Discard the bay leaves from the Crock Pot.
8. Mix the shredded pork with pan juices.

9. For burgers, spread ketchup evenly over the inside of each burger bun.

10. Divide lettuce, followed by shredded pork, tomato, and onion slices.

11. Serve immediately.

**Nutritional Information (Per Serving)**
Calories: 537
Fat: 34.4 g
Sat Fat: 12.3 g
Carbohydrates: 25.7 g
Fiber: 3.4 g
Sugar: 8.6 g
Protein: 39.8 g
Sodium: 583 mg

# Pork Chops with Spice Rub

**Servings:** 4
**Cooking Time:** 4 hours
**Ingredients:**
1 pound pork chops
½ tablespoons dried rosemary
½ tablespoon curry powder
½ tablespoon fennel seeds
½ teaspoon salt
½ tablespoon dried thyme
½ tablespoon fresh chives, chopped
½ tablespoon ground cumin
2 tablespoons olive oil
½ cup beef broth

**Directions:**
1. Pour half the oil into the Crock Pot.
2. In a bowl, mix the rest of the ingredients except the pork chops and broth, and rub it all over the chops.
3. Add broth to the pot, place the chops in it, and close the lid.
4. Set the pot on High and cook for 4 hours.

**Nutritional Information (Per Serving)**
Calories: 438
Fat: 35.8 g
Sat Fat: 11.7 g
Carbohydrates: 1.8 g
Fiber: 0.9 g
Sugar: 0.2 g
Protein: 26.5 g
Sodium: 468 mg

# Roasted Leg of Lamb

**Servings:** 10
**Cooking Time:** 8 hours
**Ingredients:**
2 tablespoons olive oil
5 garlic cloves, minced
1 tablespoon fresh rosemary, minced
1 tablespoon fresh thyme, minced
2 teaspoons lemon zest, grated
1 teaspoon red pepper flakes, crushed
1 teaspoon cayenne pepper
½ teaspoon ground cumin
Salt and pepper to taste
1 (3 lb.) boneless leg of lamb
½ cup chicken broth
2 tablespoons fresh lemon juice

**Directions:**
1. In a bowl, add oil, garlic, herbs, lemon zest, and spices, and mix until well combined.

2. Rub the lamb generously with the oil mixture.

3. In a large Crock Pot, place the lamb leg. Pour broth and lemon juice evenly on top.

4. Set the Crock Pot on Low. Cover and cook for about 8 hours.

**Nutritional Information (Per Serving)**
Calories: 286
Fat: 13 g
Sat Fat: 9.5 g
Carbohydrates: 1.3 g
Fiber: 0 g
Sugar: 0 g
Protein: 38.7 g

# Mustard Rosemary Lamb

**Servings:** 6
**Cooking Time:** 8 hours
**Ingredients:**
3 pounds leg of lamb
3 tablespoons whole-grain mustard
6 sprigs thyme
1¼ teaspoons dried rosemary
Salt and pepper to taste
2 tablespoons olive oil
½ cup beef broth
A handful fresh mint leaves
1½ teaspoons garlic, minced

**Directions:**
1. Score the lamb at 4–5 places. Place garlic and rosemary in the slits.

2. Place in the Crock Pot. Rub oil over it. Sprinkle mustard, salt, and pepper over it and rub it well.

3. Add the broth and close the lid.

4. Set the pot on Low and cook for 8 hours. Add thyme and mint during the last hour of cooking.

**Nutritional Information (Per Serving)**
Calories: 371
Fat: 16.4 g
Sat Fat: 4.8 g
Carbohydrates: 2.5 g
Fiber: 1 g
Sugar: 0.5 g
Protein: 47.9 g

# Balsamic Lamb Leg

**Servings:** 2
**Cooking Time:** 8 hours
**Ingredients:**
2 pounds lamb leg
1 sprig fresh rosemary
Salt to taste
3 tablespoons balsamic vinegar
2 cloves garlic, minced
1 head lettuce
1 cup water

**Directions:**
1. Place lamb in the Crock Pot.
2. Add the rest of the ingredients except lettuce into a bowl and mix well. Pour over the lamb.
3. Close the lid. Set the pot on Low and cook for 8 hours or on High for 4 hours.
4. Remove the lamb with a slotted spoon and place it on your cutting board. When cool enough to handle, shred the lamb with a pair of forks.
5. Add the lamb back into the pot. Stir well. Cook for 10 minutes without the lid.
6. Place the lettuce leaves on a serving platter. Spoon the lamb on it and serve.

**Nutritional Information (Per Serving)**
Calories: 632
Fat: 20.4 g
Sat Fat: 8 g
Carbohydrates: 6.2 g
Fiber: 1.2 g
Sugar: 1.7 g
Protein: 93 g

# Braised Lamb

**Servings:** 4
**Cooking Time:** 6 hours
**Ingredients:**
4 lamb shanks (keep the fat on)
1 Vidalia onion, diced
2 carrots, peeled and chopped
2 stalks of celery, chopped
3 garlic cloves, chopped
2 tomatoes, chopped
2 cups beef stock
2 tablespoons of olive oil
1 cup red wine
1 bay leaf
1 teaspoon fresh thyme, chopped
Salt and pepper to taste

**Directions:**
1. Season the lamb with salt and pepper, and cook in the olive oil in a large pan over medium-high heat. Cook for five minutes on each side until the outsides are brown.

2. Meanwhile, place the onion, carrots, celery, garlic, tomatoes, thyme, and bay leaf into the Crock Pot. Place the cooked lamb on top of the vegetables in the pot.

3. Take the frying pan off the heat. Add the wine and simmer, scraping the bits of cooked lamb off the bottom of the frying pan. Add the drippings to the slow cooker.

4. Cook on High for six hours.

**Nutritional Information (Per Serving)**
Calories: 557
Fat: 26.5 g
Sat Fat: 8.2 g
Carbohydrates: 29.8 g

Fiber: 6.4 g
Sugar: 10.9 g
Protein: 35.7 g

# Moroccan Lamb Stew

**Servings:** 6
**Cooking Time:** 8 hours
**Ingredients:**
2 pounds lamb, cut into chunks
2 large sweet potatoes, diced
1 green pepper, chopped
4 tablespoons Ras El Hanout Spice Blend
1 cup dried apricots, diced
2 tomatoes, chopped
3 tablespoons butter
2 cups coconut milk
Salt to taste

**Directions:**
1. Heat a sauce pan over medium heat and roast the spice blend. Add the lamb and mix well with the spice blend.
2. Add the butter to sear the lamb, then transfer it to a Crock Pot.
3. Add the rest of the ingredients, and cook on low for 8 hours.
4. Serve with your favorite vegetable.

**Nutritional Information (Per Serving)**
Calories: 583
Fat: 36.2 g
Sat Fat: 24.6 g
Carbohydrates: 20.8 g
Fiber: 4.4 g
Sugar: 8.9 g
Protein: 46.1 g

# Venison Steak and Veggies

**Servings:** 4

**Cooking Time:** 3–6 hours

**Ingredients:**

4 venison steaks, 8 ounces each

1 onion, chopped

1 eggplant, chopped

2 carrots, chopped

3 cloves garlic, chopped

Salt and pepper to taste

1 cup red wine

**Directions:**

1. Season venison with salt and pepper and place in the Crock Pot.

2. Top with onion, eggplant, carrots, and garlic.

3. Pour red wine over the ingredients and cook on Low for 6 hours or on High for 3 hours.

**Nutritional Information (Per Serving)**

Calories: 346

Fat: 2.5 g

Sat Fat: 0 g

Carbohydrates: 14.6 g

Fiber: 5.4 g

Sugar: 6.6 g

Protein: 51.1 g

# CHAPTER SIX

# Fish and Seafood

## Indonesian Fish

**Servings:** 6

**Cooking Time:** 5 hours

**Ingredients:**

1 large onion, sliced

4 tablespoons fresh lime juice

3 pounds fish steak (use halibut or swordfish)

3 tablespoons soy sauce

Salt to taste

Crushed red pepper flakes to taste

2 tablespoons olive oil

½ teaspoon ground pepper

1 teaspoon ground coriander

**Directions:**

1. Add half the onions, soy sauce, lime juice, coriander, crushed red pepper, salt, pepper, and olive oil into a bowl and mix well. Place the fish pieces in it. Turn the fish so that it is well coated.

2. Sprinkle the rest of the onions over the fish. Cover the bowl with cling wrap.

3. Place the bowl in the refrigerator for 3–4 hours.

4. Transfer the ingredients into the Crock Pot.

5. Close the lid. Set the pot on High and cook for 2 hours.

6. Transfer to a serving platter. Pour the cooking liquid over the fish and serve.

**Nutritional Information (Per Serving)**

Calories: 208
Fat: 12.7 g
Sat Fat: 2.7 g
Carbohydrates: 4.3 g
Fiber: 0.7 g
Sugar: 1.5 g
Protein: 19.9 g

# Seafood Stew

**Servings:** 6

**Cooking Time:** 6 hours 45 minutes

**Ingredients:**

28 ounces crushed tomatoes

3 cups vegetable broth

1½ cups white wine

3 minced garlic cloves

1 pound potatoes cut into chunks

½ cup diced onion

1 teaspoon basil

1 teaspoon thyme

¼ teaspoon red pepper flakes

⅛ teaspoon cayenne pepper

Salt and pepper to taste

2 pounds seafood (shrimp, crab legs, or firm whitefish)

**Directions:**

1. Place all ingredients, except for the seafood, in the Crock Pot and stir.

2. Cook on Low for 6 hours. Make sure the potatoes are done.

3. Add the seafood, and set the temperature on High.

4. Cook for another 45 minutes, but check on the seafood after 30 minutes. You don't want to overcook.

**Nutritional Information (Per Serving)**

Calories: 490

Fat: 3.4 g

Sat Fat: 1 g

Carbohydrates: 32.7 g

Fiber: 6.4 g

Sugar: 10.8 g

Protein: 41.7 g

# Poached Salmon

**Servings:** 8
**Cooking Time:** 1½ hours
**Ingredients:**
4 cups water
2 bay leaves
2 teaspoons black peppercorns
8 salmon fillets
4 sprigs rosemary
2 cloves garlic, minced
2 teaspoons kosher salt
Freshly ground pepper and salt to taste
2 lemons, thinly sliced

To serve:
Lemon wedges
Olive oil
Coarse sea salt

**Directions:**
1. Add water, bay leaves, black peppercorns, rosemary, and garlic into the pot.

2. Close the lid. Set the pot on High and cook for 30 minutes.

3. Sprinkle salt and pepper over the salmon and place in the Crock Pot.

4. Set the pot on High and cook for 1 hour. Keep a check on the salmon after 45 minutes of cooking. Cook until done.

5. Remove the salmon with a slotted spoon and place it on a serving platter.

6. Sprinkle with sea salt and drizzle oil, and serve with lemon wedges.

**Nutritional Information (Per Serving)**

Calories: 242
Fat: 11.1 g
Sat Fat: 1.6 g
Carbohydrates: 2 g
Fiber: 0.6 g
Sugar: 0.4 g
Protein: 34.8 g

# Salmon with Wine Sauce

**Servings:** 6
**Cooking Time:** 1 hour
**Ingredients:**
1 cup dry white wine
1½ cups water
1 shallot, sliced thinly
1 lemon, sliced thinly
¼ cup fresh dill, chopped finely
Salt and pepper to taste
6 (4 oz.) salmon fillets

**Directions:**
1. In a Crock Pot, mix all ingredients except salmon fillets.
2. Place salmon fillets on top, skin side down.
3. Set the Crock Pot on Low. Cover and cook for 1–2 hours.

**Nutritional Information (Per Serving)**
Calories: 192
Fat: 7.1 g
Sat Fat: 1 g
Carbohydrates: 3.4 g
Fiber: 0 g
Sugar: 0 g
Protein: 22.6 g

# Citrus Salmon

**Servings:** 4
**Cooking Time:** 1 hour 30 minutes
**Ingredients:**
2 pounds wild salmon with skin
2 cups water
1 cup freshly squeezed orange juice
1 lemon, sliced thin
1 shallot, sliced
1 bay leaf
6 sprigs fresh Italian parsley
1 teaspoon black pepper
1 teaspoon sea salt
¼ cup olive oil

**Directions:**
1. Combine water, orange juice, lemons, shallot, bay leaf, and parsley in the Crock Pot and heat on high for 30 minutes.

2. Sprinkle salt and pepper on salmon and place in the pot, skin side down. Drizzle with olive oil.

3. Cook on Low for 1 hour.

**Nutritional Information (Per Serving)**
Calories: 408
Fat: 20.6 g
Sat Fat: 3.1 g
Carbohydrates: 8.7 g
Fiber: 0.7 g
Sugar: 5.6 g
Protein: 46.1 g
Sodium: 623 mg

# Shrimp Scampi

**Servings:** 3

**Cooking Time:** 2 hours 40 minutes

**Ingredients:**

¼ cup chicken broth

½ cup vermouth

3 diced garlic cloves

2 tablespoons olive oil

1 teaspoon chopped parsley

1 pound raw shrimp

**Directions:**

1. Place all ingredients in the Crock Pot and stir.

2. Cook for 2½ hours on low or 1½ hours on high.

3. Use a tong or slotted spoon to transfer the shrimp to individual plates or bowls.

4. Spoon the broth over the shrimp.

**Nutritional Information (Per Serving)**

Calories: 310

Fat: 12 g

Sat Fat: 2.1 g

Carbohydrates: 3.7 g

Fiber: 0.1 g

Sugar: 0.1 g

Protein: 35 g

Sodium: 436 mg

# Polenta with Shrimp

**Servings:** 6
**Cooking Time:** 8 hours
**Ingredients:**
*For Polenta:*
2 cups cornmeal
4 cups water
4 cups milk
Salt to taste
½ cup shredded Cheddar cheese

*For Shrimp:*
1 lb. uncooked peeled and deveined shrimp without tails
¼ cup olive oil
2 tablespoons lemon juice
2 minced garlic cloves
Salt and pepper to taste
If you like extra heat, add 1 teaspoon chili powder

**Directions:**
1. Add the cornmeal to the Crock Pot.
2. Pour the water and milk into a pan, and bring to boil.
3. Pour the hot liquid over the cornmeal.
4. Stir in the salt, and combine well.
5. Cook for 8 hours on Low or 4 hours on High.
6. Add the shredded cheese, and stir until it melts. Turn off the slow cooker, but keep the polenta warm.
7. Combine all the shrimp ingredients in a bowl and combine.
8. Refrigerate the shrimp for 15 minutes.
9. Add the shrimp to a skillet, and brown on each side for 4 minutes.
10. Transfer the polenta to a plate, and top with the shrimp.

**Nutritional Information (Per Serving)**

Calories: 430
Fat: 17.6 g
Sat Fat: 5.8 g
Carbohydrates: 40.9 g
Fiber: 3 g
Sugar: 7.7 g
Protein: 28.3 g
Sodium: 339 mg

# Spicy Shrimp

**Servings:** 4
**Cooking Time:** 4 hours
**Ingredients:**
1 pound shrimp, shelled and deveined
2 stalks celery, diced
1 small onion, chopped
1 red bell pepper, chopped
28 ounces diced tomatoes
1 clove garlic, minced
¼ teaspoon black pepper
¼ teaspoon white pepper
½ teaspoon red pepper flakes
5 drops of tabasco sauce
Salt to taste

**Directions:**
1. Combine all ingredients in the Crock Pot except for the shrimp.

2. Cook 3 hours on high and stir all the ingredients together.

3. Add shrimp and cook for 1 more hour. If you're looking for something hot to go with a salad, this makes an excellent pairing. If shrimp is not your favorite seafood, you can substitute it for other types of fish.

**Nutritional Information (Per Serving)**
Calories: 191
Fat: 2.5 g
Sat Fat: 0.7 g
Carbohydrates: 14.1 g
Fiber: 3.5 g
Sugar: 7.6 g
Protein: 28.2 g

# Lemon Pepper Tilapia with Asparagus

**Servings:** 8
**Cooking Time:** 3 hours
**Ingredients:**
8 tilapia fillets
20 asparagus spears, chopped
8 teaspoons lemon-pepper seasoning or to taste
4 tablespoons butter
½ cup lemon juice

**Directions:**
1. Take 8 foils. Lay the fillets in the middle of the foil. Sprinkle 1 teaspoon lemon pepper seasoning over it.

2. Place ½ tablespoon of butter on each of the fillets. Divide and place asparagus over the fish.

3. Wrap foil all around the fish. Seal it well.

4. Place the packets in the Crock Pot. It can be overlapped while placing it.

5. Close lid. Set the pot on High and cook for 2 hours if thawed and 3 hours if frozen.

**Nutritional Information (Per Serving)**
Calories: 182
Fat: 8.5 g
Sat Fat: 4.8 g
Carbohydrates: 4 g
Fiber: 1.9 g
Sugar: 1.5 g
Protein: 23.7 g
Sodium: 376 mg

# Fish Curry

**Servings:** 8
**Cooking Time:** 4 hours
**Ingredients:**
2 tablespoons ginger, minced
3 tablespoons curry powder
3 tablespoons olive oil
1 teaspoon ground cinnamon
4 cloves garlic, minced
1 teaspoon turmeric powder
1 teaspoon chili powder
1 bell pepper, finely chopped
1 chili pepper, chopped
2 tomatoes, chopped
1 cup water
3 pounds tilapia, cubed
Salt to taste

**Directions:**
1. Add all the ingredients except tilapia into the Crock Pot and stir.
2. Close the lid. Set the pot on Low and cook for 4 hours. Add tilapia during the last 45 minutes of cook time.
3. Stir and serve.

**Nutritional Information (Per Serving)**
Calories: 213
Fat: 7.4 g
Sat Fat: 1.5 g
Carbohydrates: 5.8 g
Fiber: 1.9 g
Sugar: 1.8 g
Protein: 32.7 g

# Lemon Herbed Tilapia

**Servings:** 6
**Cooking Time:** 1½ hours
**Ingredients:**
6 (4 oz.) skinless tilapia fillets
Salt and pepper to taste
½ cup onion, chopped
2 teaspoons fresh lemon rind, grated
2 tablespoons fresh parsley, chopped
2 tablespoons fresh dill, chopped
2 tablespoon unsalted butter, melted
1 lemon, cut into wedges

**Directions:**
1. Grease a Crock Pot with butter-flavored cooking spray.
2. Sprinkle the tilapia fillets generously with salt and pepper.
3. Arrange the tilapia fillets in the bottom of the Crock Pot.
4. Place onion, lemon rind, and parsley evenly over fillets. Drizzle with melted butter.
5. Set the Crock Pot on High. Cover and cook for about 1½ hours.
6. Serve these fillets with lemon slices.

**Nutritional Information (Per Serving)**
Calories: 153
Fat: 5.9 g
Sat Fat: 2.9 g
Carbohydrates: 3.2 g
Fiber: 1.1 g
Sugar: 0 g
Protein: 24.5 g

# Chinese-Style Salmon

**Servings:** 4
**Cooking Time:** 3 hours
**Ingredients:**
4 10-oz. salmon fillets
2 cups frozen mixed Asian vegetables
Salt and pepper to taste
2 tablespoons soy sauce
2 tablespoons honey
1½ tablespoons lemon juice

**Directions:**
1. Place the vegetables inside the Crock Pot.
2. Salt and pepper the salmon fillets.
3. Lay the salmon on top of the vegetables.
4. Stir the remaining ingredients together in a bowl, and pour on the salmon.
5. Cook for 3 hours on High.
6. Serve with white rice. Drizzle the cooking juices over the salmon.

**Nutritional Information (Per Serving)**
Calories: 441
Fat: 17.7 g
Sat Fat: 2.7 g
Carbohydrates: 15.2 g
Fiber: 1.2 g
Sugar: 10.7 g
Protein: 56.7 g
Sodium: 591 mg

# Spicy Seafood Stew

**Servings:** 2
**Cooking Time:** 6 hours
**Ingredients:**
½ cup chicken broth
1 small bell pepper, chopped
1 small onion, chopped
7 ounces canned diced tomatoes
1 clove garlic, minced
4 ounces tomato sauce
Hot pepper sauce to taste
½ cup water
1 bay leaf
2 tablespoons olive oil
¼ teaspoon Cajun seasoning
1½ teaspoons dried thyme
3 ounces shrimp, peeled, deveined
4 ounces fish fillets, skinless, cut into 1-inch pieces
A handful fresh parsley, chopped, to garnish

**Directions:**
1. Add all the ingredients except seafood to the Crock Pot. Mix well.

2. Close the lid. Set the pot on Low and cook for 6 hours or on High for 3 hours.

3. Add the seafood during the last 30 minutes of cooking and stir.

4. Stir occasionally while it is cooking.

5. Ladle into soup bowls. Garnish with parsley and serve.

**Nutritional Information (Per Serving)**
Calories: 394
Fat: 22.7 g
Sat Fat: 4 g

Carbohydrates: 28 g
Fiber: 6 g
Sugar: 9.7 g
Protein: 22.8 g
Sodium: 919 mg

# Lemon Pepper Cod with Asparagus

**Servings:** 4
**Cooking Time:** 2 hours
**Ingredients:**
1 pound fresh cod filets
1 bundle of asparagus
2 lemons
4 teaspoons black pepper, divided
4 teaspoons white pepper, divided
4 tablespoons butter, divided.

**Directions:**
1. Place each fish filet on a piece of foil. Cover with asparagus. Sprinkle with peppers and then squeeze the juice from half a lemon onto each fish filet.

2. Add one tablespoon of butter to each piece of fish and then wrap the foil around the fish until it is completely sealed.

3. Place the 4 packets in the Crock Pot.

4. Cook on high for 2 hours.

**Nutritional Information (Per Serving)**
Calories: 226
Fat: 12.8 g
Sat Fat: 7.4 g
Carbohydrates: 8 g
Fiber: 3.3 g
Sugar: 2 g
Protein: 22.6 g
Sodium: 157 mg

# CHAPTER SEVEN

# Soups

## Kale Chicken Soup

**Servings:** 4
**Cooking Time:** 6 hours
**Ingredients:**
1 pound chicken thighs
1 sprig fresh thyme
1 tablespoon fresh thyme, chopped
Salt and pepper to taste
1 clove garlic, minced
2½ cups chicken broth
1 tablespoon olive oil
1 medium onion, chopped
2 cups packed kale, discard hard stems and ribs, chopped

**Directions:**
1. Sprinkle salt and pepper over the chicken and place in the Crock Pot.

2. Sprinkle garlic over the chicken. Add chicken broth, oil, and thyme sprig and stir.

3. Close the lid. Set the pot on High and cook for 4 hours. Remove the chicken with a slotted spoon and place it on your cutting board. When cool enough to handle, shred with a pair of forks. Discard the thyme.

4. Add the bones back into the Crock Pot. Refrigerate the chicken.

5. Add the rest of the ingredients.

6. Cover and cook on High for 2 hours.

7. Discard the bones and add chicken into the pot during the last 10 minutes of cooking.

8. Ladle into soup bowls and serve.

**Nutritional Information (Per Serving)**
Calories: 300
Fat: 12.8 g
Sat Fat: 3.1 g
Carbohydrates: 7.4 g
Fiber: 1.4 g
Sugar: 1.6 g
Protein: 37.3 g

# Jalapeño Popper Soup

**Servings:** 6
**Cooking Time:** 3 hours
**Ingredients:**
1½ tablespoons butter
1 small onion, chopped
1–2 jalapeños, deseed if desired, chopped
½ small green pepper, chopped
Salt and pepper to taste
¾ pound chicken breast, skinless, boneless
1½ cups chicken broth
1 large clove garlic, minced
¼ pound bacon, cooked until crisp, crumbled
¼ teaspoon paprika
6 tablespoons cheddar cheese, shredded
6 tablespoons Monterrey Jack cheese, shredded
3 ounces cream cheese
¼ cup heavy whipping cream
½ teaspoon ground cumin

**Directions:**
1. Place a saucepan with butter over medium heat. Add onion, jalapeño, green pepper, salt, and pepper. Sauté for 2–3 minutes and transfer into the Crock Pot.
2. Add chicken and broth.
3. Close the lid. Set the pot on High and cook for 3 hours.
4. When done, remove chicken with a slotted spoon and place it on your cutting board. Shred chicken with a fork and add it back into the pot.
5. Add the rest of the ingredients and stir until cheese melts.
6. Ladle into soup bowls and serve.

**Nutritional Information (Per Serving)**

Calories: 334
Fat: 24.1 g
Sat Fat: 11.8 g
Carbohydrates: 3 g
Fiber: 0.5 g
Sugar: 1 g
Protein: 25.2 g

# Cabbage Roll Soup

**Servings:** 6
**Cooking Time:** 3 hours
**Ingredients:**
2 tablespoons olive oil
¼ cup onion, chopped
2 shallots, chopped
1¼ pounds ground beef
½ teaspoon salt
2 cloves garlic, minced
½ teaspoon dried oregano
½ teaspoon dried parsley
½ teaspoon pepper powder
12 ounces marinara sauce
1 cup cauliflower, grated to a rice-like texture
3 cups beef broth
6 cups cabbage, thinly sliced

**Directions:**
1. Add oil into a saucepan and place over medium heat.
2. Add onions and shallots and sauté until translucent.
3. Stir in ground beef. Sauté until it is brown.
4. Add spices, salt, and dried herbs. Sauté for a few seconds until fragrant. Transfer into the Crock Pot.

5. Add marinara sauce and mix well. Add cauliflower and stir until well combined.

6. Add beef broth and cabbage and stir well.

7. Close the lid. Set the pot on High and cook for 3 hours

8. Ladle into soup bowls and serve.

**Nutritional Information (Per Serving)**
Calories: 313
Fat: 12.9 g
Sat Fat: 3.5 g
Carbohydrates: 14.8 g
Fiber: 3.9 g
Sugar: 8.2 g
Protein: 33.7 g
Sodium: 889 mg

# Vegetable Soup

**Servings:** 10
**Cooking Time:** 6 hours
**Ingredients:**
2 large sweet potatoes, peeled and diced
2 pounds carrots, peeled and diced
2 red onions, chopped
1 head of garlic, peeled
20 ounces spinach, fresh and rinsed
1 pound frozen peas, thawed
2 cups chicken or beef stock
Salt and pepper to taste

**Directions:**
1. Place the vegetables into the crock pot and cover with the stock.

2. Sprinkle some salt and pepper on top, then add more later if necessary.

3. Cook on Low for 6 hours. This chunky soup can be pureed after it cooks if you prefer something smoother.

**Nutritional Information (Per Serving)**
Calories: 151
Fat: 0.6 g
Sat Fat: 0.1 g
Carbohydrates: 32.5 g
Fiber: 8.3 g
Sugar: 8.1 g
Protein: 5.8 g

# Beef Bone Broth

**Servings:** 6
**Cooking Time:** 10 hours
**Ingredients:**
4 pounds beef bones
2 carrots, chopped
6 cloves garlic, minced
2 stalks of celery, chopped
2 bay leaves
1 teaspoon salt
2 teaspoons apple cider vinegar

**Directions:**
1. Place the vegetables in the Crock Pot, followed by the beef bones and bay leaves.
2. Add the salt, vinegar, and enough water just to cover the bones.
3. Cook on low for 10 hours.
4. Discard the bones before serving the soup.

**Nutritional Information (Per Serving)**
Calories: 20
Fat: 0.2 g
Sat Fat: 0.1 g
Carbohydrates: 3.2 g
Fiber: 0.7 g
Sugar: 1.1 g
Protein: 1.3 g
Sodium: 668 mg

# Pizza Soup

**Servings:** 4

**Cooking Time:** 6–7 hours

**Ingredients:**

½ pound Italian sausage

8 ounces canned crushed tomatoes

1 can (16 ounces) mushrooms or an equal amount of fresh mushrooms

1 small onion, chopped

¼ pound pepperoni, thinly sliced

1 teaspoon dried oregano

1 cup beef broth

1 small green pepper, chopped

½ teaspoon garlic powder

1 teaspoon Italian seasoning

4 tablespoons mozzarella cheese, freshly grated

2 tablespoons Parmesan cheese, grated

**Directions:**

1. Place a skillet with sausage over medium heat. Cook until brown. Drain excess fat and transfer sausage into the Crock Pot.

2. Add the rest of the ingredients except both cheese and stir.

3. Close the lid. Set the pot on Low and cook for 6–7 hours.

4. Ladle into soup bowls. Garnish with both the cheese and serve.

**Nutritional Information (Per Serving)**
Calories: 480
Fat: 35 g
Sat Fat: 13 g
Carbohydrates: 11 g
Fiber: 3.6 g
Sugar: 5.5 g
Protein: 30.1 g

Sodium: 1557 mg

# Taco Soup

**Servings:** 4
**Cooking Time:** 6 hours
**Ingredients:**
1 pound ground beef
1 tablespoon butter, melt
1 tablespoon taco seasoning
10 ounces canned diced tomatoes
4 ounces cream cheese
2 cups chicken broth
Salt and pepper to taste
2 tablespoons Cheddar cheese, shredded to garnish
Cilantro to garnish

**Directions:**
1. Place a skillet with butter and beef over medium heat. Cook until brown and transfer into the Crock Pot.

2. Add the rest of the ingredients except Cheddar and cilantro, and mix well.

3. Close the lid. Set the pot on Low and cook for 6 hours.

4. Ladle into soup bowls and serve garnished with Cheddar and cilantro.

**Nutritional Information (Per Serving)**
Calories: 396
Fat: 21.8 g
Sat Fat: 11.7 g
Carbohydrates: 7 g
Fiber: 0.9 g
Sugar: 3 g
Protein: 40.5 g

# Cauliflower and Ham Soup

**Servings:** 5
**Cooking Time:** 2½ hours
**Ingredients:**
12 ounces cauliflower florets
1 cup water
3 cups chicken broth
½ teaspoon onion powder
¼ teaspoon garlic powder
1½ cups ham, chopped
2 teaspoons fresh thyme leaves, chopped
1 tablespoon apple cider vinegar
1 tablespoon butter
Salt and pepper to taste

**Directions:**
1. Add cauliflower, onion powder, garlic powder, water, and broth into the Crock Pot.
2. Close the lid. Set the pot on Low and cook for 4 hours or until cauliflower is soft.
3. Blend with an immersion blender until smooth.
4. Add ham and thyme leaves. Cover and cook on High for 30 minutes.
5. Add butter, salt, pepper, and apple cider vinegar and stir.
6. Ladle into soup bowls and serve.

**Nutritional Information (Per Serving)**
Calories: 129
Fat: 6.7 g
Sat Fat: 2.9 g
Carbohydrates: 6.3 g
Fiber: 2.4 g
Sugar: 2.2 g
Protein: 11.1 g

# Bacon Soup

**Servings:** 6
**Cooking Time:** 6 hours
**Ingredients:**
2 tablespoons butter
4 medium jalapeño peppers, seeded and chopped
1 teaspoon dried thyme, crushed
½ teaspoon ground cumin
½ teaspoon ground coriander
3½ cups chicken broth
6 ounces cheddar cheese, shredded
Salt and pepper to taste
2 bacon slices, cooked and chopped

**Directions:**
1. In a soup pan, melt butter over medium heat. Add jalapeño peppers, and sauté for about 1–2 minutes. Transfer to the Crock Pot.
2. Add the herbs and chicken broth, and stir.
3. Close the lid. Set the pot on Low and cook for 6 hours.
4. Blend with an immersion blender until smooth.
5. Stir in cheddar cheese, heavy cream, salt, and pepper. Cover and cook on High for 20-30 minutes.
6. Serve hot with a topping of bacon.

**Nutritional Information (Per Serving)**
Calories: 210
Fat: 16.9 g
Sat Fat: 9.5 g
Carbohydrates: 1.9 g
Fiber: 0.5 g
Sugar: 0.9 g
Protein: 12.5 g

# Chicken Noodle Soup

**Servings:** 6
**Cooking Time:** 6 hours
**Ingredients:**
3 tablespoons coconut oil
1½ cups celery, chopped
9 green onions, green parts only, chopped
1½ pounds chicken thighs, skinless, boneless
9 cups chicken stock
¾ teaspoon dried oregano
1 teaspoon dried basil
3 cups spiralized daikon noodles
Freshly ground pepper to taste

**Directions:**
1. Using a spiralizer, make noodles of the daikon. Use 3 cups of the daikon noodles.

2. Place a skillet with oil over medium heat. Add chicken and cook until brown on both sides. Transfer into the Crock Pot.

3. Add the rest of the ingredients except daikon noodles and stir.

4. Close the lid. Set the pot on Low and cook for 6 hours.

5. When done, remove chicken with a slotted spoon and place it on your work area. When cool enough to handle, shred the chicken with a pair of forks and add it back into the pot. Stir and heat thoroughly.

6. Add noodles and stir.

7. Ladle into soup bowls and serve.

**Nutritional Information (Per Serving)**
Calories: 330
Fat: 24.7 g
Sat Fat: 11.1 g
Carbohydrates: 4.6 g
Fiber: 1.6 g

Sugar: 2.4 g
Protein: 22.1 g
Sodium: 1259 mg

# CHAPTER EIGHT

# Snacks and Dessert

## Artichoke and Spinach Dip

**Servings:** 20
**Cooking Time:** 4 hours
**Ingredients:**

1 package frozen spinach thawed and with all the liquid squeezed out

1 can artichoke hearts—drained and chopped into quarters

½ cup sour cream

½ cup Alfredo sauce

Salt and pepper to taste

1 cup shredded Swiss cheese

**Directions:**

1. Mix all the ingredients in a Crock Pot.

2. Cook for 4 hours on High.

3. Serve with French bread cubes or cut vegetables.

**Nutritional Information (Per Serving)**

Calories: 59
Fat: 4.2 g
Sat Fat: 2.2 g
Carbohydrates: 3 g
Fiber: 0.5 g
Sugar: 0.2 g
Protein: 2.6 g
Sodium: 209 mg

# Mushrooms in Wine Sauce

**Servings:** 10
**Cooking Time:** 8 hours
**Ingredients:**
2 cups chicken broth
½ cup red wine
½ teaspoon garlic powder
½ teaspoon Worcestershire sauce
2 pounds fresh mushrooms
2 tablespoons butter, melt

**Directions:**
1. Place the mushrooms in the bottom of the Crock Pot.
2. Pour in the liquids, Worcestershire sauce, and garlic powder. Stir to combine.
3. Add the butter.
4. Cook for 8 hours on Low.

**Nutritional Information (Per Serving)**
Calories: 58
Fat: 2.8 g
Sat Fat: 1.5 g
Carbohydrates: 3.7 g
Fiber: 0.9 g
Sugar: 1.9 g
Protein: 3.9 g
Sodium: 178 mg

# Buffalo Chicken Wings

**Servings:** 8
**Cooking Time:** 5 hours
**Ingredients:**
1½ pounds chicken wings
1 tablespoon butter, melted
⅓ cup Ranch dressing
12 ounces chicken wing sauce
1 teaspoon hot sauce or to taste

**Directions:**
1. Add butter, chicken wing sauce, and hot sauce into the Crock Pot and mix well.
2. Add chicken wings and stir until well coated.
3. Close the lid. Set the pot on Low and cook for 4–5 hours or on High for 2–2½ hours.
4. Serve hot or warm with blue cheese dressing.

**Nutritional Information (Per Serving)**
Calories: 218
Fat: 15 g
Sat Fat: 4.7 g
Carbohydrates: 3.6 g
Fiber: 0 g
Sugar: 0.3 g
Protein: 15.9 g
Sodium: 1216 mg

# Buffalo Chicken Dip

**Servings:** 6

**Cooking Time:** 1½ hours

**Ingredients:**

4 ounces cream cheese, softened, cubed

1 cup mozzarella cheese, shredded

2 ounces blue cheese, crumbled

1½ cups deli rotisserie chicken, diced

½ cup sour cream

½ tablespoon Ranch seasoning

2 tablespoons jalapeños (optional), to top

2 green onions, thinly sliced + extra to garnish

½ cup hot sauce + extra to serve

**Directions:**

1. Spray the inside of the Crock Pot with cooking spray.

2. Add all the ingredients into the Crock Pot and mix well.

3. Close the lid. Set the pot on High and cook for 1½ hours.

4. Serve warm garnished with jalapeños, hot sauce, and green onions.

5. Serve with celery sticks or keto crackers.

**Nutritional Information (Per Serving)**

Calories: 232

Fat: 17.8 g

Sat Fat: 9.9 g

Carbohydrates: 3.5 g

Fiber: 0.2 g

Sugar: 0.8 g

Protein: 15.4 g

Sodium: 940 mg

# Lemon Garlic Chicken Kebabs

**Servings:** 4

**Cooking Time:** 3-4 hours

**Ingredients:**

¾ pound chicken thighs, skinless, boneless, cut into 2-inch pieces

1 tablespoon garlic, minced

½ teaspoon salt

3 tablespoons fresh lemon juice

½ teaspoon dried oregano

3 tablespoons olive oil

4 bamboo skewers

**Directions:**

1. Add all the cooking ingredients except chicken into a zip lock bag and shake well.

2. Add chicken and shake well. Let it marinate for 60–90 minutes.

3. Trim the bamboo skewers to fit into your Crock Pot. Thread the chicken onto the skewers.

4. Place in the Crock Pot. Cover and set the pot on High.

5. Cook for 3–4 hours. Check after 3 hours of cooking.

**Nutritional Information (Per Serving)**

Calories: 261

Fat: 22.6 g

Sat Fat: 4.6 g

Carbohydrates: 1.1 g

Fiber: 0.2 g

Sugar: 0.3 g

Protein: 14.5 g

Sodium: 458 mg

# Apple Cake

**Servings:** 8

**Cooking Time:** 2½ hours

**Ingredients:**

2 cups white flour

½ cup brown sugar

2 teaspoons cinnamon

1 teaspoon baking soda

½ teaspoon baking powder

Dash of salt

Dash of cloves

1 cup applesauce

½ cup buttermilk

⅓ cup butter

2 tablespoons vanilla

1 large egg

2 cups chopped dried apple

2 cups whipped topping

**Directions:**

1. Coat a Crock Pot with a nonstick spray.

2. Line the bottom and sides with parchment paper, leaving a bit on top to lift out the cake.

3. Coat the parchment paper with the nonstick spray.

4. Stir together all the dry ingredients and spices in a bowl.

5. Melt the butter in a saucepan.

6. In another bowl, stir together the melted butter, applesauce, egg, buttermilk, and vanilla.

7. Add the applesauce mixture to the flour, and mix thoroughly for a smooth batter.

8. Stir in the dried apples.

9. Transfer the batter into the Crock Pot and level out the top.

10. Cook for 2½ hours on High.

11. Slice the cake, and serve warm with whipped topping.

**Nutritional Information (Per Serving)**
Calories: 323
Fat: 12.2 g
Sat Fat: 7.3 g
Carbohydrates: 47.6 g
Fiber: 2.9 g
Sugar: 20.2 g
Protein: 5.3 g
Sodium: 282 mg

# Pumpkin Custard

**Servings:** 6

**Cooking Time:** 3 hours

**Ingredients:**

15 ounces pumpkin puree

4 eggs, beaten

½ cup heavy cream

2 teaspoons pumpkin pie spice

2 teaspoons vanilla extract

4 tablespoons sugar

½ teaspoon salt

⅓ cup whipped cream

**Directions:**

1. Grease 6 ramekins.

2. In a large bowl, add all ingredients except whipped cream, and beat until smooth.

3. Divide mixture evenly in prepared ramekins. Cover them with foil.

4. Pour about 2 cups water into the Crock Pot. Place a rack in it. Place the ramekins on the rack.

5. Close the lid. Set the pot on High and cook for 3 hours, or until set.

6. Remove the ramekins from the pot, and place them on a wire rack to cool.

7. Serve warm or cold with a topping of whipped cream.

**Nutritional Information (Per Serving)**

Calories: 156

Fat: 9 g

Sat Fat: 4.6 g

Carbohydrates: 15 g

Fiber: 2.1 g

Sugar: 10.8 g

Protein: 4.9 g
Sodium: 245 mg

# Chocolate Pudding Cake

**Servings:** 8
**Cooking Time:** 2½ hours
**Ingredients:**
1 cup white flour
½ cup chocolate milk
⅓ cup sugar
2 tablespoons cocoa powder
1½ teaspoon baking powder
2 tablespoons olive oil
2 teaspoons vanilla
½ cup semisweet chocolate chips
½ cup chopped peanuts
¾ cup sugar
2 tablespoons unsweetened cocoa powder

**Directions:**
1. Coat the inside of the Crock Pot with a nonstick cooking spray.

2. In one bowl, mix the flour, sugar, and baking powder. Stir in the milk, olive oil, and vanilla.

3. Add the chocolate chips and peanuts. Stir very well to combine.

4. Pour the batter into the pot.

5. In the second bowl, mix the sugar and cocoa powder. Stir in 3 cups of boiling water. Pour the liquid on top of the batter.

6. Cook for 2½ hours on High.

7. Let cool.

8. Distribute the pudding cake into a bowl and serve with ice cream.

**Nutritional Information (Per Serving)**
Calories: 334
Fat: 13 g
Sat Fat: 4.2 g
Carbohydrates: 53.3 g
Fiber: 2.9 g
Sugar: 36.6 g
Protein: 5 g
Sodium: 12 mg

# Peach Cobbler

**Servings:** 8
**Cooking Time:** 3 hours
**Ingredients:**
4 cups peaches, peeled and sliced
¾ cup sugar
1 cup biscuit mix
1 cup milk

**Directions:**
1. Coat a Crock Pot with a nonstick cooking spray.
2. In a bowl, toss the peaches with ¼ cup of sugar.
3. Place the peaches in the pot.
4. In another bowl, stir together the biscuit mix, milk, and the remaining sugar.
5. Top the peaches with the mixture.
6. Cook for 3 hours on High.
7. Serve with whipped topping or ice cream.

**Nutritional Information (Per Serving)**
Calories: 176
Fat: 3 g
Sat Fat: 1 g
Carbohydrates: 36.3 g
Fiber: 1.5 g
Sugar: 28.8 g
Protein: 2.8 g
Sodium: 196 mg

# Warm Fruit Compote

**Servings:** 10
**Cooking Time:** 6 hours
**Ingredients:**
2 apples, peeled and sliced
½ cup dried cranberries
1 cup raisins
1 cup dried apricots, cut in half
8 ounces canned pineapple, unsweetened
8 ounces canned peaches, unsweetened
1 cup freshly squeezed orange juice
1 cinnamon stick
1 cup slivered almonds

**Directions:**
1. Place the cinnamon stick on the bottom of your Crock Pot.
2. Add all the fruits and pour the orange juice over the top.
3. Cook on low for 6 hours.
4. Serve with slivered almonds on top.

**Nutritional Information (Per Serving)**
Calories: 168
Fat: 5.1 g
Sat Fat: 0.4 g
Carbohydrates: 31.1 g
Fiber: 4 g
Sugar: 22.9 g
Protein: 3.2 g
Sodium: 4 mg

# Fruit and Honey

**Servings:** 10
**Cooking Time:** 2–4 hours
**Ingredients:**
4 ripe plums, cut into wedges with pits removed
3 pears, cut into wedges with core removed
3 apples, cored and cut into chunks
½ cup dried apricots, cut in half
¼ cup melted butter
¼ cup natural honey
8 ounce can of orange segments, no sugar added
8 ounce can of pineapple chunks, no sugar added
1 cup chopped walnuts

**Directions:**
1. Pour the pineapple and orange pieces, with their liquid, into the Crock Pot.

2. Add plums, pears, apples, and dried apricots.

3. Pour the melted butter over the fruit and give it a toss, then drizzle the honey.

4. Cook on Low for 4 hours or High for 2 hours.

5. Sprinkle with walnuts before serving.

**Nutritional Information (Per Serving)**
Calories: 248
Fat: 12.3 g
Sat Fat: 3.3 g
Carbohydrates: 35.2 g
Fiber: 5 g
Sugar: 27.2 g
Protein: 3.9 g
Sodium: 35 mg

# Conclusion

If you want to enjoy healthy homemade meals but don't have the time to cook, a Crock Pot works wonders. I hope you enjoy the delicious Crock Pot recipes in this book. When in need, just use your Crock Pot.

Happy cooking!

Finally, I want to thank you for reading my book. If you enjoyed the book, please share your thoughts and post a review on the book retailer's website. It would be greatly appreciated!

Best wishes,

Melanie Bennet

www.ingramcontent.com/pod-product-compliance
Lightning Source LLC
Chambersburg PA
CBHW052033150726

48002CB00002B/589